Flinn Scientific
ChemTopic™ Labs

The Gas Laws

Senior Editor

Irene Cesa
Flinn Scientific, Inc.
Batavia, IL

Curriculum Advisory Board

Bob Becker
Kirkwood High School
Kirkwood, MO

Kathleen J. Dombrink
McCluer North High School
Florissant, MO

Robert Lewis
Downers Grove North High School
Downers Grove, IL

John G. Little
St. Mary's High School
Stockton, CA

Lee Marek
Naperville North High School
Naperville, IL

John Mauch
Braintree High School
Braintree, MA

Dave Tanis
Grand Valley State University
Allendale, MI

FLINN SCIENTIFIC INC.
"Your Safer Source for Science Supplies"
P.O. Box 219 • Batavia, IL 60510
1-800-452-1261 • www.flinnsci.com

ISBN 1-877991-77-5

Copyright © 2003 Flinn Scientific, Inc.

All rights reserved. No part of this book may be reproduced or transmitted in any form or by any means, electronic or mechanical, including, but not limited to photocopy, recording, or any information storage and retrieval system, without permission in writing from Flinn Scientific, Inc. No part of this book may be included on any Web site.

Reproduction permission is granted only to the science teacher who has purchased this volume of Flinn ChemTopic™ Labs, The Gas Laws, Catalog No. AP6367 from Flinn Scientific, Inc. Science teachers may make copies of the reproducible student pages for use only by their students.

Permission to reprint copyrighted materials is gratefully acknowledged:
Life on Planet V, © 1997 Robert Becker,
Cartesian Diver-Sions, © 1994 Robert Becker.
Reproduced for one-time use with permission from Robert Becker. All Rights Reserved.

Printed in the United States of America.

Table of Contents

	Page
Flinn ChemTopic™ Labs Series Preface	i
About the Curriculum Advisory Board	ii
The Gas Laws Preface	iii
Format and Features	iv–v
Experiment Summaries and Concepts	vi–vii

Experiments

Boyle's Law in a Bottle	1
Charles's Law and Absolute Zero	17
Molar Volume of Hydrogen	31
Technology and the Forgotten Gas Law	43
Life on Planet V	57

Demonstrations

The Collapsing Can	61
Massing Gases	63
Molar Mass of Butane	67
Diffusion of Gases	70
Construction of Gas Volume Cubes	73
Cartesian Divers	75

Supplementary Information

Safety and Disposal Guidelines	78
National Science Education Standards	80
Master Materials Guide	82

Flinn ChemTopic™ Labs Series Preface
Lab Manuals Organized Around Key Content Areas in Chemistry

In conversations with chemistry teachers across the country, we have heard a common concern. Teachers are frustrated with their current lab manuals, with experiments that are poorly designed and don't teach core concepts, with procedures that are rigid and inflexible and don't work. Teachers want greater flexibility in their choice of lab activities. As we further listened to experienced master teachers who regularly lead workshops and training seminars, another theme emerged. Master teachers mostly rely on collections of experiments and demonstrations they have put together themselves over the years. Some activities have been passed on like cherished family recipe cards from one teacher to another. Others have been adapted from one format to another to take advantage of new trends in microscale equipment and procedures, technology innovations, and discovery-based learning theory. In all cases the experiments and demonstrations have been fine-tuned based on real classroom experience.

Flinn Scientific has developed a series of lab manuals based on these "cherished recipe cards" of master teachers with proven excellence in both teaching students and training teachers. Created under the direction of an Advisory Board of award-winning chemistry teachers, each lab manual in the Flinn ChemTopic™ Labs series contains 4–6 student-tested experiments that focus on essential concepts and applications in a single content area. Each lab manual also contains 4–6 demonstrations that can be used to illustrate a chemical property, reaction, or relationship and will capture your students' attention. The experiments and demonstrations in the Flinn ChemTopic™ Labs series are enjoyable, highly focused, and will give students a real sense of accomplishment.

Laboratory experiments allow students to experience chemistry by doing chemistry. Experiments have been selected to provide students with a crystal-clear understanding of chemistry concepts and encourage students to think about these concepts critically and analytically. Well-written procedures are guaranteed to work. Reproducible data tables teach students how to organize their data so it is easily analyzed. Comprehensive teacher notes include a master materials list, solution preparation guide, complete sample data, and answers to all questions. Detailed lab hints and teaching tips show you how to conduct the experiment in your lab setting and how to identify student errors and misconceptions before students are led astray.

Chemical demonstrations provide another teaching tool for seeing chemistry in action. Because they are both visual and interactive, demonstrations allow teachers to take students on a journey of observation and understanding. Demonstrations provide additional resources to develop central themes and to magnify the power of observation in the classroom. Demonstrations using discrepant events challenge student misconceptions that must be broken down before new concepts can be learned. Use demonstrations to introduce new ideas, illustrate abstract concepts that cannot be covered in lab experiments, and provide a spark of excitement that will capture student interest and attention.

Safety, flexibility, and choice

Safety always comes first. Depend on Flinn Scientific to give you upfront advice and guidance on all safety and disposal issues. Each activity begins with a description of the hazards involved and the necessary safety precautions to avoid exposure to these hazards. Additional safety, handling, and disposal information is also contained in the teacher notes.

The selection of experiments and demonstrations in each Flinn ChemTopic™ Labs manual gives you the flexibility to choose activities that match the concepts your students need to learn. No single teacher will do all of the experiments and demonstrations with a single class. Some experiments and demonstrations may be more helpful with a beginning-level class, while others may be more suitable with an honors class. All of the experiments and demonstrations have been keyed to national content standards in science education.

Chemistry is an experimental science!

Whether they are practicing key measurement skills or searching for trends in the chemical properties of substances, all students will benefit from the opportunity to discover chemistry by doing chemistry. No matter what chemistry textbook you use in the classroom, Flinn ChemTopic™ Labs will help you give your students the necessary knowledge, skills, attitudes, and values to be successful in chemistry.

About the Curriculum Advisory Board

Flinn Scientific is honored to work with an outstanding group of dedicated chemistry teachers. The members of the Flinn ChemTopic Labs Advisory Board have generously contributed their proven experiments, demonstrations, and teaching tips to create these topic lab manuals. The wisdom, experience, creativity, and insight reflected in their lab activities guarantee that students who perform them will be more successful in learning chemistry. On behalf of all chemistry teachers, we thank the Advisory Board members for their service to the teaching profession and their dedication to the field of chemistry education.

Bob Becker teaches chemistry and AP chemistry at Kirkwood High School in Kirkwood, MO. Bob received his B.A. from Yale University and M.Ed. from Washington University and has 16 years of teaching experience. A well-known demonstrator, Bob has conducted more than 100 demonstration workshops across the U.S. and Canada and is currently a Team Leader for the Flinn Foundation Summer Workshop Program. His creative and unusual demonstrations have been published in the *Journal of Chemical Education,* the *Science Teacher,* and *Chem13 News.* Bob is the author of two books of chemical demonstrations, *Twenty Demonstrations Guaranteed to Knock Your Socks Off, Volumes I and II,* published by Flinn Scientific. Bob has been awarded the James Bryant Conant Award in High School Teaching from the American Chemical Society, the Regional Catalyst Award from the Chemical Manufacturers Association, and the Tandy Technology Scholar Award.

Kathleen J. Dombrink teaches chemistry and advanced-credit college chemistry at McCluer North High School in Florissant, MO. Kathleen received her B.A. in Chemistry from Holy Names College and M.S. in Chemistry from St. Louis University and has more than 31 years of teaching experience. Recognized for her strong support of professional development, Kathleen has been selected to participate in the Fulbright Memorial Fund Teacher Program in Japan and NEWMAST and Dow/NSTA Workshops. She served as co-editor of the inaugural issues of *Chem Matters* and was a Woodrow Wilson National Fellowship Foundation Chemistry Team Member for more than 11 years. Kathleen is currently a Team Leader for the Flinn Foundation Summer Workshop Program. Kathleen has received the Presidential Award, the Midwest Regional Teaching Award from the American Chemical Society, the Tandy Technology Scholar Award, and a Regional Catalyst Award from the Chemical Manufacturers Association.

Robert Lewis teaches chemistry and AP chemistry at Downers Grove North High School in Downers Grove, IL. Robert received his B.A. from North Central College and M.A. from University of the South and has more than 26 years of teaching experience. He was a founding member of Weird Science, a group of chemistry teachers that has traveled throughout the country to stimulate teacher interest and enthusiasm for using demonstrations to teach science. Robert was a Chemistry Team Leader for the Woodrow Wilson National Fellowship Foundation and is currently a Team Leader for the Flinn Foundation Summer Workshop Program. Robert has received the Presidential Award, the James Bryant Conant Award in High School Teaching from the American Chemical Society, the Tandy Technology Scholar Award, a Regional Catalyst Award from the Chemical Manufacturers Association, and a Golden Apple Award from the State of Illinois.

John G. Little teaches chemistry and AP chemistry at St. Mary's High School in Stockton, CA. John received his B.S. and M.S. in Chemistry from University of the Pacific and has more than 36 years of teaching experience. Highly respected for his well-designed labs, John is the author of two lab manuals, *Chemistry Microscale Laboratory Manual* (D.C. Heath), and *Microscale Experiments for General Chemistry* (with Kenneth Williamson, Houghton Mifflin). He is also a contributing author to *Science Explorer* (Prentice Hall) and *World of Chemistry* (McDougal Littell). John served as a Chemistry Team Leader for the Woodrow Wilson National Fellowship Foundation from 1988 to 1997 and is currently a Team Leader for the Flinn Foundation Summer Workshop Program. He has been recognized for his dedicated teaching with the Tandy Technology Scholar Award and the Regional Catalyst Award from the Chemical Manufacturers Association.

Lee Marek retired from teaching chemistry at Naperville North High School in Naperville, IL and currently works at the University of Illinois—Chicago. Lee received his B.S. in Chemical Engineering from the University of Illinois and M.S. degrees in both Physics and Chemistry from Roosevelt University. He has more than 31 years of teaching experience and is currently a Team Leader for the Flinn Foundation Summer Workshop Program. His students have won national recognition in the International Chemistry Olympiad, the Westinghouse Science Talent Search, and the Internet Science and Technology Fair. Lee was a founding member of ChemWest, a regional chemistry teachers alliance, and led this group for 15 years. Together with two other ChemWest members, Lee also founded Weird Science and has presented 500 demonstration and teaching workshops for more than 300,000 students and teachers across the country. Lee has performed science demonstrations on the *David Letterman Show* 20 times. Lee has received the Presidential Award, the James Bryant Conant Award in High School Teaching from the American Chemical Society, the National Catalyst Award from the Chemical Manufacturers Association, and the Tandy Technology Scholar Award.

John Mauch teaches chemistry and AP chemistry at Braintree High School in Braintree, MA. John received his B.A. in Chemistry from Whitworth College and M.A. in Curriculum and Education from Washington State University and has 26 years of teaching experience. John is an expert in "writing to learn" in the chemistry curriculum and in microscale chemistry. He is the author of two lab manuals, *Chemistry in Microscale, Volumes I and II* (Kendall/Hunt). He is also a dynamic and prolific demonstrator and workshop leader. John has presented the Flinn Scientific Chem Demo Extravaganza show at NSTA conventions for eight years and has conducted more than 100 workshops across the country. John was a Chemistry Team Member for the Woodrow Wilson National Fellowship Foundation program for four years and is currently a Board Member for the Flinn Foundation Summer Workshop Program.

Dave Tanis is Associate Professor of Chemistry at Grand Valley State University in Allendale, MI. Dave received his B.S. in Physics and Mathematics from Calvin College and M.S. in Chemistry from Case Western Reserve University. He taught high school chemistry for 26 years before joining the staff at Grand Valley State University to direct a coalition for improving pre-college math and science education. Dave later joined the faculty at Grand Valley State University and currently teaches courses for pre-service teachers. The author of two laboratory manuals, Dave acknowledges the influence of early encounters with Hubert Alyea, Marge Gardner, Henry Heikkinen, and Bassam Shakhashiri in stimulating his long-standing interest in chemical demonstrations and experiments. Continuing this tradition of mentorship, Dave has led more than 40 one-week institutes for chemistry teachers and served as a Team Member for the Woodrow Wilson National Fellowship Foundation for 13 years. He is currently a Board Member for the Flinn Foundation Summer Workshop Program. Dave received the College Science Teacher of the Year Award from the Michigan Science Teachers Association.

Preface
The Gas Laws

Applications of the gas laws are important in physiology, meteorology, scuba diving, even hot-air ballooning. Boyle's law is demonstrated with every breath we take. Charles's law is illustrated in the ascent and landing of a hot-air balloon. The purpose of *The Gas Laws,* Volume 9 in the Flinn ChemTopic™ Labs series, is to provide high school chemistry teachers with laboratory activities that will help students investigate, apply, and explain the relationships among the four measurable gas properties—pressure, temperature, volume, and number of moles of gas. Five experiments and six demonstrations allow students to measure the gas properties, derive their mathematical relationships, and explain the behavior of gases under different conditions.

Pressure and Volume

The study of the gas laws begins with pressure. Take yourself back more than 350 years ago and imagine the surprise that greeted Torricelli's demonstration that the pressure of air would support a column of mercury more than 29 inches high. A few years later, Robert Boyle would compare the pressure of air to the force stored in a spring. Use "The Collapsing Can" demonstration to show your students that air pressure is indeed a force to be reckoned with! Afterwards, challenge your students with "Life on Planet V" to describe how their lives would be different if there were no air pressure. Once students understand the concept of pressure, they will be ready to investigate the first gas law, the effect of pressure on the volume of a gas, in "Boyle's Law in a Bottle." Students need only a syringe and a pressurized soda bottle to recreate Boyle's classic measurements and derive the mathematical relationship between pressure and volume. After students have finished the calculations and the graphing, they will enjoy playing with "Cartesian Divers," a classic toy that demonstrates how Boyle's law affects the density and buoyancy of a gas.

Temperature and Kinetic Energy

The temperature of a gas affects both its volume and its pressure. In "Charles's Law and Absolute Zero," students measure how the volume of a fixed amount of gas changes as the gas is heated or cooled in a flexible container at constant pressure. Graphing the results will lead students to the concept of absolute zero and to the most fundamental concept describing the behavior of matter—the kinetic-molecular theory. Alternatively, in "Technology and the Forgotten Gas Law," students use a pressure sensor and a temperature sensor to determine how the temperature of a gas affects its pressure if the volume is held constant. The resulting mathematical relationship between temperature and pressure also leads to the definition of absolute zero. In both experiments, the results can only be explained in terms of the kinetic energy of moving molecules. Use the "Diffusion of Gases" demonstration to show your students that molecules really do move and that their kinetic energy depends on temperature.

Avogadro's Law and the Number of Moles of Gas

Avogadro's law introduces the number of moles of gas as an independent variable and leads to the ideal gas law, which ties together all the measurable gas properties. According to Avogadro's law, the volume of a gas is directly proportional to the number of moles of gas if the temperature and pressure are held constant. In the microscale experiment "Molar Volume of Hydrogen," students use Avogadro's law and the ideal gas law to determine the molar volume of an ideal gas at standard temperature and pressure. Two demonstrations, "Massing Gases" and "Molar Mass of Butane" illustrate how Avogadro's law and the ideal gas law are also used to determine the molar mass of a gas. As a culminating activity, consider using "Construction of Gas Volume Cubes" to assess students understanding of the gas laws and their ability to perform ideal gas law calculations. Given an assigned number of moles of an ideal gas, students must calculate the volume of the gas at standard temperature and pressure and then construct a cube to match the volume. Assign different groups of students different numbers of moles, and the result will be a classroom exhibit of Avogadro's law!

Chemistry is an experimental science!

The overlapping selection of experiments and demonstrations in *The Gas Laws* gives you the ability to cover the topics you feel are important in the safest, most effective way possible. Depend on Flinn Scientific to provide you with up-to-date, modern variations of classic experiments and demonstrations. Remember, chemistry is an experimental science, and nowhere is this more evident that in the relationship between experiment, theory, and applications in the study of gases. Finally, no matter what experiments and demonstrations you choose, your students are assured of success. Each experiment and demonstration in *The Gas Laws* has been thoroughly tested and retested. You know they will work! Use the experiment summaries and concepts on the following pages to locate the concepts you want to teach and to choose activities that will help you meet your goals.

Format and Features

Flinn ChemTopic™ Labs

All experiments and demonstrations in Flinn ChemTopic™ Labs are printed in a 10⅞" × 11" format with a wide 2" margin on the inside of each page. This reduces the printed area of each page to a standard 8½" × 11" format suitable for copying.

The wide margin assures you the entire printed area can be easily reproduced without hurting the binding. The margin also provides a convenient place for teachers to add their own notes.

Concepts — Use these bulleted lists along with state and local standards, lesson plans, and your textbook to identify activities that will allow you to accomplish specific learning goals and objectives.

Background — A balanced source of information for students to understand why they are doing an experiment, what they are doing, and the types of questions the activity is designed to answer. This section is not meant to be exhaustive or to replace the students' textbook, but rather to identify the core concepts that should be covered before starting the lab.

Experiment Overview — Clearly defines the purpose of each experiment and how students will achieve this goal. Performing an experiment without a purpose is like getting travel directions without knowing your destination. It doesn't work, especially if you run into a roadblock and need to take a detour!

Pre-Lab Questions — Making sure that students are prepared for lab is the single most important element of lab safety. Pre-lab questions introduce new ideas or concepts, review key calculations, and reinforce safety recommendations. The pre-lab questions may be assigned as homework in preparation for lab or they may be used as the basis of a cooperative class activity before lab.

Materials — Lists chemical names, formulas, and amounts for all reagents—along with specific glassware and equipment—needed to perform the experiment as written. The material dispensing area is a main source of student delay, congestion, and accidents. Three dispensing stations per room are optimum for a class of 24 students working in pairs. To safely substitute different items for any of the recommended materials, refer to the *Lab Hints* section in each experiment or demonstration.

Safety Precautions — Instruct and warn students of the hazards associated with the materials or procedure and give specific recommendations and precautions to protect students from these hazards. Please review this section with students before beginning each experiment.

Procedure — This section contains a stepwise, easy-to-follow procedure, where each step generally refers to one action item. Contains reminders about safety and recording data where appropriate. For inquiry-based experiments the procedure may restate the experiment objective and give general guidelines for accomplishing this goal.

Data Tables — Data tables are included for each experiment and are referred to in the procedure. These are provided for convenience and to teach students the importance of keeping their data organized in order to analyze it. To encourage more student involvement, many teachers prefer to have students prepare their own data tables. This is an excellent pre-lab preparation activity—it ensures that students have read the procedure and are prepared for lab.

Post-Lab Questions or Data Analysis — This section takes students step-by-step through what they did, what they observed, and what it means. Meaningful questions encourage analysis and promote critical thinking skills. Where students need to perform calculations or graph data to analyze the results, these steps are also laid out sequentially and in order.

Format and Features

Teacher's Notes

Master Materials List — Lists the chemicals, glassware, and equipment needed to perform the experiment. All amounts have been calculated for a class of 30 students working in pairs. For smaller or larger class sizes or different working group sizes, please adjust the amounts proportionately.

Preparation of Solutions — Calculations and procedures are given for preparing all solutions, based on a class size of 30 students working in pairs. With the exception of particularly hazardous materials, the solution amounts generally include 10% extra to account for spillage and waste. Solution volumes may be rounded to convenient glassware sizes (100-mL, 250-mL, 500-mL, etc.).

Safety Precautions — Repeats the safety precautions given to the students and includes more detailed information relating to safety and handling of chemicals and glassware. Refers to Material Safety Data Sheets that should be available for all chemicals used in the laboratory.

Disposal — Refers to the current *Flinn Scientific Catalog/Reference Manual* for general guidelines and specific procedures governing the disposal of laboratory waste. Because we recommend that teachers review local regulations before beginning any disposal procedure, the information given in this section is for general reference purposes only. However, if a disposal step is included as part of the experimental procedure itself, then the specific solutions needed for disposal are described in this section.

Lab Hints — This section reveals common sources of student errors and misconceptions and where students are likely to need help. Identifies the recommended length of time needed to perform each experiment, suggests alternative chemicals and equipment that may be used, and reminds teachers about new techniques (filtration, pipeting, etc.) that should be reviewed prior to lab.

Teaching Tips — This section puts the experiment in perspective so that teachers can judge in more detail how and where a particular experiment will fit into their curriculum. Identifies the working assumptions about what students need to know in order to perform the experiment and answer the questions. Highlights historical background and applications-oriented information that may be of interest to students.

Sample Data — Complete, actual sample data obtained by performing the experiment exactly as written is included for each experiment. Student data will vary.

Answers to All Questions — Representative or typical answers to all questions. Includes sample calculations and graphs for all data analysis questions. Information of special interest to teachers only in this section is identified by the heading "Note to the teacher." Student answers will vary.

Look for these icons in the *Experiment Summaries and Concepts* section and in the *Teacher's Notes* of individual experiments to identify inquiry-, microscale-, and technology-based experiments, respectively.

Experiment Summaries and Concepts

Experiment

Boyle's Law in a Bottle—Pressure versus Volume

More than 350 years ago, Robert Boyle used air trapped in a glass tube above a column of mercury to study the relationship between the volume and pressure of air. In this experiment, students carry out a modern version of Boyle's classic experiment using only a syringe and a special, "pressurized" soda bottle. Discover Boyle's law in a safe and environmentally friendly manner!

Charles's Law and Absolute Zero—How Low Can You Go?

Charles's law was inspired by the first sensational flight in the history of hot-air ballooning. A hot-air balloon works on the principle that the volume of a gas expands when it is heated. When a gas is heated, the kinetic energy of the particles increases and they move faster. What happens when a gas is cooled? Is there a lower limit to temperature at which the particles stop moving altogether? What would happen to the volume of a gas at this minimum temperature? Find out just how low you can go in this innovative Charles's law experiment.

Molar Volume of Hydrogen—Combining the Gas Laws

The volume occupied by one mole of a gas is called the molar volume. According to the ideal gas law, the molar volume of an ideal gas is equal to 22.4 L/mole at standard temperature and pressure and is independent of the identity of the gas. In this microscale experiment, students measure the volume corresponding to a known amount of hydrogen gas and then use the gas laws to calculate its molar volume at STP.

Technology and the Forgotten Gas Law—Pressure versus Temperature

Avogadro, Boyle, and Charles—together these scientists gave us the ABC's of gas laws. Their experiments and their stories are well known to students and teachers alike. But who was Guillaume Amontons and what is his gas law? The purpose of this technology-based experiment is to measure the pressure of a gas at different temperatures and thus rediscover the forgotten gas law relating the temperature and pressure of a gas.

Life on Planet V—A Classroom Activity

Imagine that you have been relocated to Planet V, a planet just like Earth but with no atmosphere at all. What would it be like to live in a vacuum? Which of our tools and toys—from vacuum cleaners to squirt guns—would still work the same? Which would not work at all? Use this "mental lab" activity to stimulate student discussion of the concepts of pressure and vacuum.

Concepts

- Gas properties
- Pressure
- Boyle's law
- Kinetic-molecular theory

- Temperature
- Charles's law
- Absolute zero
- Kinetic-molecular theory

- Avogadro's law
- Dalton's law
- Ideal gas law
- Molar volume

- Boyle's law
- Amontons's law
- Absolute zero
- Kinetic-molecular theory

- Atmospheric pressure
- Vacuum

Flinn ChemTopic™ Labs — The Gas Laws

Experiment Summaries and Concepts

Demonstration

The Collapsing Can—Pressure Is a Force Demonstration

Pressure—we all feel it. But what is it? In the case of the surrounding air, the pressure it exerts is a force, a surprisingly strong force. Use this pressure-packed demonstration to convince your students that air is a force to be reckoned with!

Massing Gases—Avogadro's Law Demonstration

Make Avogadro proud by using his law to determine the molar mass of several gases. Equal volumes of a reference gas and an "unknown" gas will be trapped inside a syringe and their masses will be measured. By comparing their mass ratio, the molar mass of the unknown gas is determined.

Molar Mass of Butane—Ideal Gas Law Demonstration

The gas laws relate the four measurable gas properties—pressure, volume, temperature, and number of moles. By combining measurements of these properties with the mass of a given quantity of gas, we can use the gas laws to calculate the molar mass of an unknown gas, in this case the butane stored under pressure in a butane lighter.

Diffusion of Gases—Kinetic Energy Demonstration

Imagine two vehicles—a large truck and a compact car—traveling down the highway. In order for these vehicles to have the same kinetic energy, the compact car must travel much faster than the large truck. The same analogy is used in this demonstration to compare the rate of mixing of two gases at room temperature.

Construction of Gas Volume Cubes—Assessment Activity

Avogadro's law states that the volume of an ideal gas is directly proportional to the number of moles of gas if the temperature and pressure are constant. In this authentic assessment activity, students are asked to calculate the volume of a given number of moles of gas at STP. They must then build a cube to the specified gas volume. Assign different groups of students different numbers of moles, and the result is a classroom exhibit of Avogadro's law!

Cartesian Divers—Boyle's Law Activity

"Diver" toys that can be manipulated to sink or float in an enclosed pool of water have been around for centuries. The toys have been used to teach concepts of density and buoyancy. In this activity, students learn to make a variety of squeezable, sinkable Cartesian divers using just a few simple materials—and a lot of imagination!

Concepts

- Atmospheric pressure
- Kinetic-molecular theory
- Vacuum

- Avogadro's law
- Molar mass
- Buoyancy

- Dalton's law
- Ideal gas law
- Molar mass

- Diffusion
- Kinetic-molecular theory

- Avogadro's law
- Molar volume
- Ideal gas
- Standard temperature and pressure (STP)

- Density
- Buoyancy
- Boyle's law

Boyle's Law in a Bottle
Pressure versus Volume

Teacher Notes

Introduction

In 1642 Evangelista Torricelli, who had worked as an assistant to Galileo, conducted a famous experiment demonstrating that the weight of air would support a column of mercury about 30 inches high in an inverted tube. Torricelli's experiment provided the first measurement of the invisible pressure of air. Robert Boyle, a "skeptical chemist" working in England, was inspired by Torricelli's experiment to measure the pressure of air when it was compressed or expanded. The results of Boyle's experiments were published in 1662 and became essentially the first gas law—a mathematical equation describing the relationship between the volume and pressure of air. What is Boyle's law and how can it be demonstrated?

Concepts

- Gas properties
- Pressure
- Boyle's law
- Kinetic-molecular theory

Background

Robert Boyle built a simple apparatus to measure the relationship between the pressure and volume of air. The apparatus consisted of a J-shaped tube that was sealed at one end and open to the atmosphere at the other end. A sample of air was trapped in the sealed end by pouring mercury into the tube (Figure 1). In the beginning of the experiment, the height of the mercury column was equal in the two sides of the tube. The pressure of the air trapped in the sealed end was equal to that of the surrounding air, equivalent to 29.9 inches (760 mm) of mercury. When Boyle added more mercury to the open end of the tube, the air trapped in the sealed end was compressed into a smaller volume (Figure 2). The difference in height of the two columns of mercury (Δh) was due to the additional pressure exerted by the compressed air compared to the surrounding air. Boyle found that when the volume of trapped air was reduced to one-half its original volume, the additional height of the column of mercury in the open end of the tube measured 29.9 inches. The pressure exerted by the compressed air was twice as great as atmospheric pressure. The mathematical relationship between the volume of the air and the pressure it exerts was confirmed through a series of measurements.

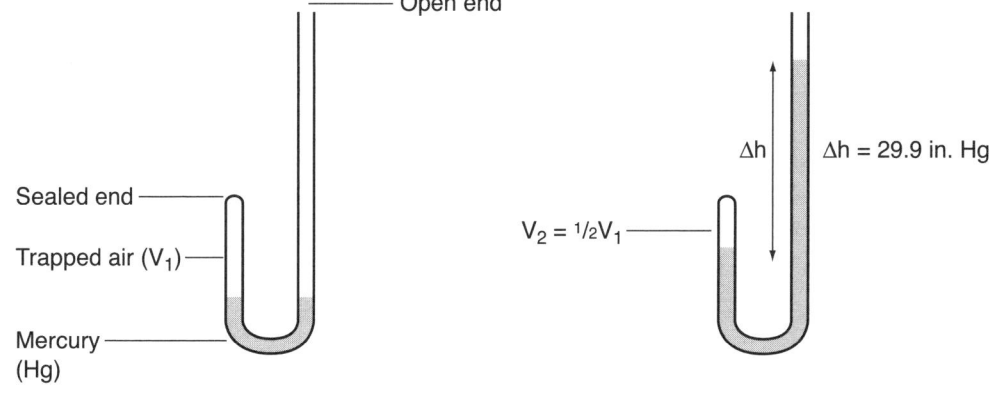

Figure 1.   **Figure 2.**

Robert Boyle, of course, is most well-known for his treatise The Sceptical Chymist *published in 1661. In this book Boyle dismantled the philosophical arguments for the "four elements" of nature and argued instead for a view of matter based on experimental evidence.*

Boyle's Law in a Bottle

Boyle's Law in a Bottle – Page 2

Teacher Notes

Experiment Overview

The purpose of this experiment is to carry out a modern version of Boyle's classic experiment. The experiment will be carried out using air trapped inside a sealed syringe within a "pressure bottle." The bottle will be pressurized by pumping in air to obtain a pressure several times greater than that of the surrounding air. As some of the excess pressure within the bottle is then released, the volume of the trapped air inside the syringe will change. Volume measurements will be made at several different pressures and the results will be analyzed by graphing to derive the mathematical relationship between pressure and volume.

Pre-Lab Questions

1. According to our modern understanding of the gas laws, there are four measurable properties (variables) of a gas. These variables are P (pressure), V (volume), T (temperature), and n (number of moles). In Boyle's experiment, which two variables were held constant?

2. Fill in the blanks to summarize the relationship among the gas properties in Boyle's experiment: For a fixed _____ of gas at constant _____, the _____ of a gas increases as the _____ of its container decreases.

3. Pressure is defined in physics as force divided by area (P = force/area). According to the kinetic-molecular theory, the particles in a gas are constantly moving and colliding with the walls of their container. The pressure of the gas is related to the total force exerted by the individual collisions. Use the kinetic theory to explain the results of Boyle's experiment.

4. The pressure scale on a tire gauge is marked in units of pounds per square inch (psi). The scale starts at zero when the gauge is exposed to the surrounding air. This means that the total pressure is equal to the gauge pressure *plus* the pressure of the surrounding air. Standard atmospheric pressure (1 atm) is equal to 14.7 psi. Assume that you have just inflated the tire on your bicycle to 82 psi using a bicycle pump. What is the total pressure of air in the tire in psi? In atmospheres?

Materials

Bicycle pump with pressure gauge, or electric air pump

Pressure bottle, 1-L, with tire valve

Syringe, 10-mL, with syringe tip cap

Barometer (optional)

Graph paper

Tire gauge (optional)

*Page 3 – **Boyle's Law in a Bottle***

Teacher Notes

Design of the Pressure Bottle

The "pressure bottle" is a 1-L PETE (polyethylene terephthalate) soda bottle. The bottle cap has been fitted with a tire valve to give an airtight seal (Figure 3). Pumping air into the bottle using an ordinary bicycle pump makes it possible to pressurize the bottle above atmospheric pressure. The bottle retains its volume when it is pressurized—any expansion is negligible. The plastic used to make these bottles will withstand pressures up to about 100 psi.

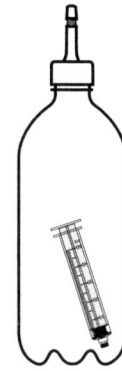

Figure 3.

Safety Precautions

The pressure bottle is safe if used properly. The bottle should not be inflated above 100 psi. Even if the bottle should explode, the plastic construction will only result in a quick release of air, an accompanying loud noise, and a hole in the bottle. The bottle will split but will not shatter. Wear eye protection (safety glasses or chemical splash goggles) when working with the pressure bottle.

Procedure

1. Using a barometer, measure the value of the local air pressure. *Note:* If a barometer is not available, consult an Internet site such as the national weather service site (http://weather.gov/) to obtain a current pressure reading for your area. Record the barometric pressure in the data table.

2. Obtain a 1-L pressure bottle and a 10-mL syringe with a rubber tip cap.

3. Press down on the brass pin in the tire valve fitted inside the bottle cap to release any excess pressure that may be inside the bottle. Remove the cap from the bottle.

4. Remove the tip cap from the syringe and pull on the plunger to draw about 9 mL of air into the syringe. Replace the tip cap to seal the air inside the syringe.

5. Place the sealed syringe inside a clean and dry, 1-L pressure bottle. Close the bottle with the special cap fitted with a tire valve. Tighten the cap securely.

6. Connect the tire valve to a bicycle pump or an electric air pump. *Note:* Exercise caution if using an electric air pump. Do not exceed the maximum suggested pressure.

7. Pump air into the pressure bottle to obtain a pressure reading of 50–60 psi on the tire gauge. Do NOT exceed 100 psi. *Note:* Using a manual pump is a safety feature—it is very difficult to pump more than about 70 psi into the pressure bottle by hand.

8. Loosen the connection between the pressure bottle–tire valve and the pump to release a small amount of pressure. As soon as you see the syringe plunger start to move, immediately retighten the tire valve to the pump.

9. Using the pump gauge, measure and record the pressure to within ±1 psi.

For best results, use a barometer to measure the local barometric pressure. The national weather service site reports corrected, sea-level air pressures. See page 38 in this lab manual for a discussion of barometric versus sea-level pressures and an equation relating them. On many syringes, the black rubber seals have two "seal lines." Make sure students are consistent in where they measure the volume! A small amount of pressure is released in step 8 before volume measurements are made—this is to overcome the friction between the rubber seal and the syringe barrel.

Boyle's Law in a Bottle

10. Measure and record the volume of air trapped in the syringe at this bottle pressure. *Note:* Measure the volume at the black rubber seal, not at the inverted V-like projection (see Figure 4). The syringe barrel has major scale divisions marked every milliliter, and minor scale divisions every 0.2 mL. The volume should be estimated to within ±0.1 mL.

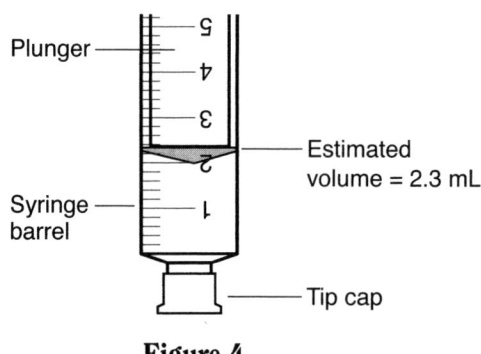

Figure 4.

11. Loosen the connection between the pressure bottle–tire valve and the bicycle pump to release a small amount of pressure from the pressure bottle. Try to reduce the pressure by no more than about 10 psi. Immediately retighten the tire valve to the pump.

12. Measure both the new pressure on the pump gauge and the new volume of the air trapped inside the syringe. Record all data in the data table. *Note:* If you are using a tire gauge to measure pressure, press lightly on the brass pin in the tire valve to release some air pressure. It may be necessary to bleed off enough air initially to get the first pressure reading below 50 psi, which is the scale maximum on many tire gauges.

13. Repeat steps 11 and 12 to measure the volume of gas trapped in the syringe at several different pressures down to about 5 psi. It should be possible to obtain at least 5–6 pressure and volume measurements in this range.

14. When the pressure on the tire gauge measures close to zero, remove the tire valve from the pump. Press down on the brass pin inside the tire valve to release all of the excess pressure within the pressure bottle. Record the final volume of air in the syringe at atmospheric pressure.

15. If time permits, repeat steps 7–14 to obtain a second, independent set of pressure–volume data. Record this data as Trial 2 in the data table.

Tire gauges come in many shapes and sizes. The best gauges for this experiment are those with an attached pressure dial rather than a "pop-out" sliding scale.

Teacher Notes

Name: _____

Class/Lab Period: _____

Boyle's Law in a Bottle

Data and Results Table

Barometric Pressure							
Trial 1				Trial 2			
Gauge Pressure	Volume of Air in Syringe	Total Pressure*	1/V†	Gauge Pressure	Volume of Air in Syringe	Total Pressure*	1/V†

*See Post-Lab Question #2.   †See Post-Lab Question #5.

Post-Lab Questions *(Use a separate sheet of paper to answer the following questions.)*

1. Convert the local barometric pressure to psi units and enter the value to the nearest psi in the Data and Results Table. Some appropriate conversion factors are shown below.

$$1 \text{ atm} = 760 \text{ mm Hg} = 29.92 \text{ in Hg} = 14.7 \text{ psi}$$

2. The pressure gauge measures the relative pressure in psi above atmospheric pressure. For each pressure reading in the Data and Results Table, add the local barometric pressure to the gauge pressure to determine the total pressure of air inside the pressure bottle. Enter the total pressure to the nearest psi in the table.

3. Plot a graph of volume on the y-axis versus total pressure on the x-axis. *Note:* The origin of the graph should be 0,0. Choose a suitable scale for each axis so that the data points fill the graph as completely as possible. Remember to label each axis and give the graph a title.

4. Describe the shape of the graph. Draw a best-fit straight or curved line, whichever seems appropriate, to illustrate how the volume of a gas changes as the pressure changes.

Boyle's Law in a Bottle

Boyle's Law in a Bottle – Page 6

5. The relationship between pressure and volume is called an "inverse" relationship—the pressure increases as the volume of air trapped in the syringe decreases. This inverse relationship may be expressed mathematically as $P \propto 1/V$. Calculate the value of $1/V$ for each volume measurement and enter the results in the Data and Results Table.

6. Plot a graph of pressure on the y-axis versus $1/V$ on the x-axis and draw a best-fit straight line through the data. *Note:* The origin of the graph should be 0,0. Choose a suitable scale for each axis so that the data points fill the graph as completely as possible.

7. Another way of expressing an inverse relationship between two variables ($P \propto 1/V$) is to say that the mathematical product of the two variables is a constant ($P \times V =$ constant). Multiply the total pressure (P) times the volume (V) for each set of data points. Construct a Results Table to summarize the $P \times V$ values.

8. Calculate the average value of the $P \times V$ "constant" and the average deviation. What is the relative percent error (uncertainty) in this constant?

    Relative percent error = (Average deviation/Average value) × 100%

9. At constant temperature, the pressure of a gas is proportional to the concentration of gas particles in the container. When some of the pressure was released from the bottle, the syringe plunger moved up. Why did this happen? Use diagrams and explain in words what happens to the gas particles moving around both inside and outside the syringe before and after the pressure is released.

10. *(Optional)* Look up the properties of PETE on the Internet. What characteristics of PETE make it an ideal plastic for use in soda bottles?

Teacher Notes

If necessary, review the definition of the average deviation with your students. The average deviation is obtained by finding the difference between each individual value and the average value, taking the sum (Σ) of their absolute values, and dividing by the number of measurements.

$$\text{average deviation} = \frac{\sum_{i=1}^{n}|x_i - \bar{x}|}{n}$$

Teacher's Notes
Boyle's Law in a Bottle

Master Materials List *(for a class of 30 students working in pairs)*

Bicycle pumps with attached pressure gauges, 5–7* or electric air pump,† 1

Barometer (optional)

Graph paper, 30 sheets

Pressure bottles, 1-L, fitted with tire valve, 5–7§

Syringes, 10-mL, with rubber septum or syringe caps, 5–7§

Tire gauges, 5–7 (optional)†

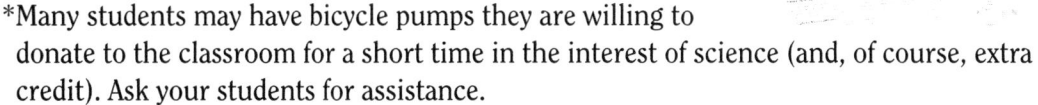

*Many students may have bicycle pumps they are willing to donate to the classroom for a short time in the interest of science (and, of course, extra credit). Ask your students for assistance.

†Electric air pumps are common items in vocational education or mechanical arts classrooms. If using an electric air pump, the teacher should inflate all of the pressure bottles ahead of time. The students may then use tire gauges to measure the pressure.

§Flinn Scientific sells a pre-made pressure bottle (Flinn Catalog No. AP5930) equipped with the attached tire valve and syringe and syringe tip cap.

Safety Precautions

The pressure bottle is safe if used properly. The bottle should not be inflated above 100 psi. Even if the bottle should explode, the plastic construction will only result in a quick release of air, an accompanying loud noise, and a hole in the bottle. The bottle will split but will not shatter. Wear eye protection (safety glasses or chemical splash goggles) when working with the pressure bottle. Teachers should inspect the pressure bottles for cracks before setting them out for student use.

Disposal

The pressure bottles and syringes are reusable—no disposal required.

Lab Hints

- The laboratory work for this experiment can reasonably be completed in about 20 minutes. This should allow ample time in a normal 50-minute class period for students to share equipment, which minimizes the investment needed for this experiment.

- Best results are obtained using a bicycle pump with an attached pressure gauge. If enough bicycle pumps cannot be rounded up with student help, the experiment may be done using common automobile tire gauges. The teacher should prepare the syringe/bottle assemblies and pressurize the bottles ahead of time. Since the scale maximum on many tire gauges is 50 psi, students may have to bleed off enough air initially to get the pressure below 50 psi. The units shown on some pressure gauges may be psig (gauge pressure per square inch. The correct units for the "total pressures" calculated in the Data and Results Table are psia (pounds per square inch absolute) rather than psi.

What does a pressure of 14.7 psi feel like? The "Atmosphere Bar" available from Flinn Scientific (AP5882) is a 52-inch steel bar that weighs 14.7 lbs. The base of the bar is one inch square. The resulting pressure of 14.7 pounds per square inch certainly feels impressive!

Teacher's Notes

- Students may need instruction in how to use a tire gauge. Students usually are too tentative—they tend to press the tire gauge softly against the valve, which allows air to escape and does not give an accurate pressure reading. The best advice is to work quickly and deliberately. There is an obvious value for students in learning to use a tire gauge so that they can inflate their automobile tires to the proper pressure. Maintaining proper tire pressure improves safety, tire wear, and gas mileage.

- Try not to exceed the maximum pressure recommended in the *Procedure* section. It was found that the graph of P versus 1/V became nonlinear as the pressure bottle was pressurized above about 70 psi (total pressure 85 psi). This can be used as a teaching point—deviations from ideal gas behavior are more important at higher pressures. Many textbooks show graphs of real versus ideal gas behavior as a function of pressure. For many gases, deviations from ideal behavior become significant at pressures greater than about 200 atm. Even at modest pressures, however, small deviations are common in the P × V "constant." Some of this deviation may also be due to a change in temperature. Compressing the gas will increase the temperature of the gas.

- This lab provides excellent data and is a great way to introduce the use of computer spreadsheet or graphical analysis programs. Using these programs, it is possible with just a "click of the mouse" to draw best-fit, straight or curved lines (trendlines) through data and obtain regression equations. High-school students are not expected to do the math involved in generating a best-fit straight line (linear regression). It is worthwhile, however, for students to learn how this important statistical tool is used to evaluate the reliability of results.

- See the *Supplementary Information* section for an example of how the data from this experiment can be analyzed to extrapolate the value of the atmospheric pressure in units of psi.

- For convenience in shipping and handling, the Flinn Pressure Bottle (Catalog No. AP5930) is prepared using a 1-L plastic soda bottle. Pressure bottles may also be prepared using more readily available 2-L soda bottles. See the *Supplementary Information* section for instructions on how to prepare home-made pressure bottles.

Teaching Tips

- As mentioned in the Introduction, Boyle's law was inspired by Torricelli's measurement of the "invisible" pressure of air. In his original paper, Boyle compared the pressure of air to the force stored in a spring. Many students may be unaware of the force exerted by the air all around them. Demonstrate the power of the invisible pressure of air using the classic "Collapsing Can" demonstration in the *Demonstrations* section of this Flinn ChemTopic™ Labs manual. After the demonstration, use the activity "Life on the Planet V" to challenge your students to imagine how their lives would be different if there were no air pressure.

- Does Boyle's law depend on the nature of the gas? The experiment can be extended to test the behavior of gases other than air by filling the syringes with pure gases such as helium, hydrogen, and nitrogen. Any source of gas may be used. Call or write us at Flinn Scientific to obtain a complimentary copy of our ChemFax No. 10527, "Construction of a Simple Gas Delivery Apparatus."

Teacher Notes

- Boyle's law can also be demonstrated with every breath you take! When you inhale, your diaphragm moves down, and the volume of the body cavity surrounding the lungs expands. As the volume increases, the pressure decreases, and the outside air, which is at a higher pressure, rushes into the lungs. The opposite occurs when you exhale—the diaphragm moves upward, the lung cavity contracts, and the pressure increases relative to the outside air, pushing air out of the lungs. See the "Functioning Lung Model" (Catalog No. FB1110) available from Flinn Scientific for a large, demonstration-size model of the pressure-volume relationship involved in breathing.

- The great 17th century physicist Isaac Newton was a contemporary of Robert Boyle, and Boyle's results prompted Newton to propose an explanation for the pressure of a gas. Newton assumed that the particles in a gas were motionless (static) and that the pressure of a gas was due to the mutual repulsion of gas particles. That no less a person than the "father of physics" and the discoverer of the calculus proposed this model might serve as a cautionary tale for all teachers—our modern, obvious explanations for gas behavior may not always be obvious to students.

- The foundation of the modern kinetic-molecular theory of gases is usually attributed to Daniel Bernoulli. In 1734 Bernoulli proposed that a gas was composed of "hard" (inelastic) particles that were in constant and random motion. The force exerted by these particles as they collided with the walls of their container was the source of the gas pressure. Using this model, Bernoulli derived a mathematical equation for the pressure of a gas. His mathematical treatment correctly "predicted" the inverse pressure-volume relationship that had been observed empirically by Robert Boyle. The development of the kinetic theory culminated in the mid-1800s with the definition of temperature and the relationship between temperature and kinetic energy.

Answers to Pre-Lab Questions *(Student answers will vary.)*

1. According to our modern understanding of the gas laws, there are four measurable properties (variables) of a gas. These variables are P (pressure), V (volume), T (temperature), and n (number of moles). In Boyle's experiment, which two variables were held constant?

    Both the temperature (T) and the number of moles of gas (n) were held constant in Boyle's J-tube experiment.

2. Fill in the blanks to summarize the relationship among the gas properties in Boyle's experiment:

    *For a fixed **number of moles** of gas at constant **temperature**, the **pressure** of a gas increases as the **volume** of its container decreases.*

Teacher's Notes

3. Pressure is defined in physics as force divided by area (P = force/area). According to the kinetic-molecular theory, the particles in a gas are constantly moving and colliding with the walls of their container. The pressure of the gas is related to the total force exerted by the individual collisions. Use the kinetic theory to explain the results of Boyle's experiment.

    In Boyle's experiment, the pressure of air increased when it was compressed into a smaller volume container. According to the kinetic theory, confining the gas particles in a smaller volume will increase the number of collisions and hence the total force of the collisions with the container walls. (The distance the particles must travel between collisions decreases as the volume is reduced.)

4. The pressure scale on a tire gauge is marked in units of pounds per square inch (psi). The scale starts at zero when the gauge is exposed to the surrounding air. This means that the total pressure is equal to the gauge pressure *plus* the pressure of the surrounding air. Standard atmospheric pressure (1 atm) is equal to 14.7 psi. Assume that you have just inflated the tire on your bicycle to 82 psi using a bicycle pump. What is the *total pressure* of air in the tire in psi? In atmospheres?

    Relative (gauge) pressure = Total pressure − Atmospheric pressure

    82 psi = Total pressure − 14.7 psi

    Total pressure = (82 + 14.7) psi = 97 psi (two significant figures)

    Convert to atm: $97 \text{ psi} \times \dfrac{1 \text{ atm}}{14.7 \text{ psi}} = 6.6 \text{ atm}$

Teacher Notes

Sample Data

Student data will vary.

Data and Results Table

Barometric Pressure				29.9 inches Hg = 15 psi			
Trial 1				**Trial 2**			
Gauge Pressure	Volume of Air in Syringe	Total Pressure*	1/V†	Gauge Pressure	Volume of Air in Syringe	Total Pressure*	1/V†
42 psi	2.0 mL	57 psi	0.50 mL^{-1}	54 psi	1.6 mL	69 psi	0.63 mL^{-1}
35 psi	2.4 mL	50 psi	0.42 mL^{-1}	35 psi	2.4 mL	50 psi	0.42 mL^{-1}
22 psi	3.3 mL	37 psi	0.30 mL^{-1}	23 psi	3.2 mL	38 psi	0.31 mL^{-1}
17 psi	3.8 mL	32 psi	0.26 mL^{-1}	14 psi	4.4 mL	29 psi	0.23 mL^{-1}
11 psi	5.0 mL	26 psi	0.20 mL^{-1}	6 psi	6.2 mL	21 psi	0.16 mL^{-1}
6 psi	6.2 mL	21 psi	0.16 mL^{-1}	3 psi	7.3 mL	18 psi	0.14 mL^{-1}
1 psi	8.4 mL	16 psi	0.12 mL^{-1}	0 psi	9.0 mL	15 psi	0.11 mL^{-1}

*See Post-Lab Question #2.   † See Post-Lab Question #5.

Answers to Post-Lab Questions *(Student answers will vary.)*

1. Convert the local barometric pressure to psi units and enter the value to the nearest psi in the Data and Results Table. Some appropriate conversion factors are shown below.

$$1 \text{ atm} = 760 \text{ mm Hg} = 29.92 \text{ in Hg} = 14.7 \text{ psi}$$

$$29.9 \text{ in Hg} \times \frac{14.7 \text{ psi}}{29.92 \text{ in Hg}} = 15 \text{ psi (rounded to the nearest psi)}$$

2. The pressure gauge measures the relative pressure in psi above atmospheric pressure. For each pressure reading in the Data and Results Table, add the local barometric pressure to the gauge pressure to determine the total pressure of air inside the pressure bottle. Enter the total pressure to the nearest psi in the table.

Sample calculation for Trial 1: Total pressure = 42 psi + 15 psi = 57 psi

Refer to the Data and Results Table for the results of the other calculations.

Teacher's Notes

3. Plot a graph of volume on the y-axis versus total pressure on the x-axis. *Note:* The origin of the graph should be 0,0. Choose a suitable scale for each axis so that the data points fill the graph as completely as possible. Remember to label each axis and give the graph a title.

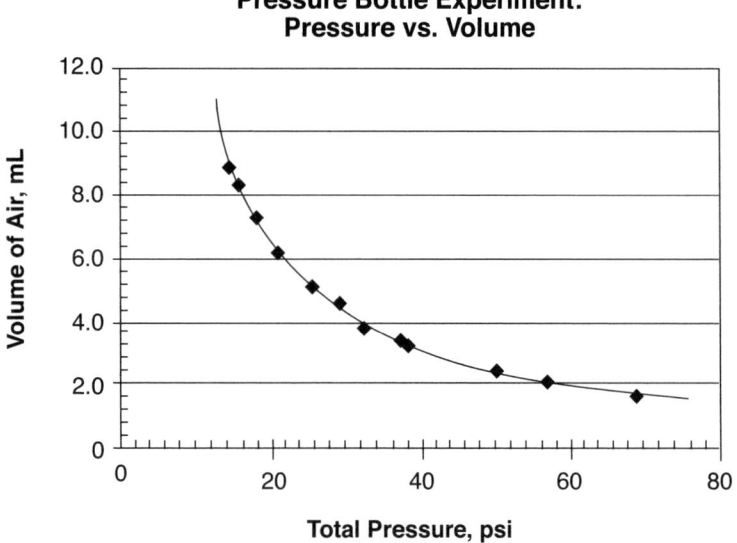

4. Describe the shape of the graph. Draw a best-fit straight or curved line, whichever seems appropriate, to illustrate how the volume of a gas changes as the pressure changes.

    The graph is curved. The volume decreases as the pressure increases. At first, there is a sharp reduction in the volume as the pressure increases. The decrease in volume then becomes more gradual and the volume appears to level off as the pressure increases further. Mathematically, the shape of the curve is described as hyperbolic. A hyperbolic curve of this type is obtained when there is an inverse relationship between two variables ($y \propto 1/x$). See the graph for the best-fit curved line through the data.

5. The relationship between pressure and volume is called an "inverse" relationship—the pressure increases as the volume of air trapped in the syringe decreases. This inverse relationship may be expressed mathematically as $P \propto 1/V$. Calculate the value of $1/V$ for each volume measurement and enter the results in the Data and Results Table.

    Sample calculation for Trial 1: $V = 2.0 \text{ mL}$
    $1/V = 0.50 \text{ mL}^{-1}$

    Refer to the Sample Data and Results Table for the results of the other calculations.

Teacher's Notes

6. Plot a graph of pressure on the y-axis versus 1/V on the x-axis and draw a best-fit straight line through the data. *Note:* The origin of the graph should be 0,0. Choose a suitable scale for each axis so that the data points fill the graph as completely as possible.

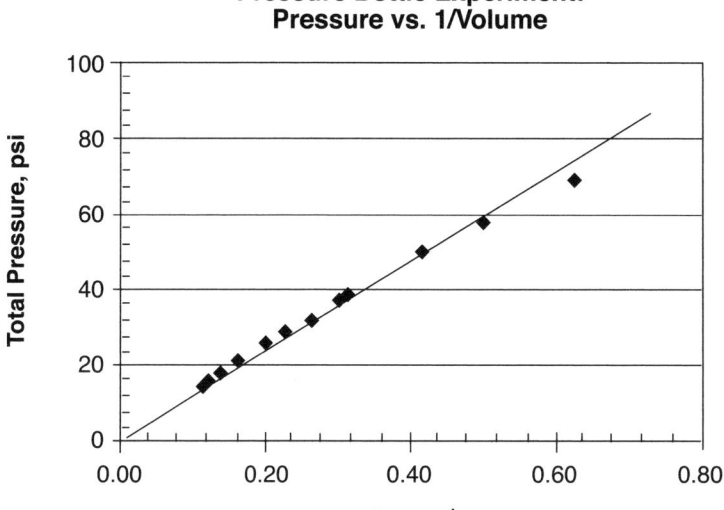

7. Another way of expressing an inverse relationship between two variables ($P \propto 1/V$) is to say that the mathematical product of the two variables is a constant ($P \times V$ = constant). Multiply the total pressure (P) times the volume (V) for each set of data points. Construct a Results Table to summarize the $P \times V$ values.

Sample Results Table

	Trial 1			Trial 2	
P (psi)	V (mL)	P × V (psi · mL)	P (psi)	V (mL)	P × V (psi · mL)
57	2.0	110	69	1.6	110
50	2.4	120	50	2.4	120
37	3.3	120	38	3.2	120
32	3.8	120	29	4.4	130
26	5.0	130	21	6.2	130
21	6.2	130	18	7.3	130
16	8.4	130	15	9.0	140
Average Value					120
Average Deviation					6

Boyle's Law in a Bottle

Teacher's Notes

8. Calculate the average value of the P × V "constant" and the average deviation. What is the relative percent error (uncertainty) in this constant?

   Relative percent error = (Average deviation/Average value) × 100%

   Average value of the (P × V) constant = 120 psi · mL

   Average deviation = 6 psi · mL

   Relative percent error = (6 psi · mL/120 psi · mL) × 100% = 5%

   It appears that the mathematical product (P × V) is a constant within plus-or-minus 5%.

9. At constant temperature, the pressure of a gas is proportional to the concentration of gas particles in the container. When some of the pressure was released from the pressure bottle, the syringe plunger moved up. Why did this happen? Use diagrams and explain in words what happens to the gas particles moving around both inside and outside the syringe before and after the pressure is released.

   Initially, the pressure was the same both inside and outside the syringe. This means there were equal concentrations of gas particles colliding with the inside and outside of the plunger, so the plunger stayed in place (A). When some of the pressure from the bottle was released, some air particles escaped, leaving fewer air particles to collide on the outside of the plunger (B). The concentration of particles inside the syringe overpowered those outside the syringe and pushed the plunger outward (the volume increased). As the volume increased, the particle concentration inside the syringe decreased. When the concentration of particles (pressure) inside the syringe was the same as that outside the syringe, the plunger stopped moving (C).

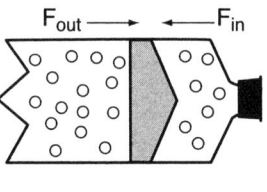
A
Equal Forces
Initial Conditions

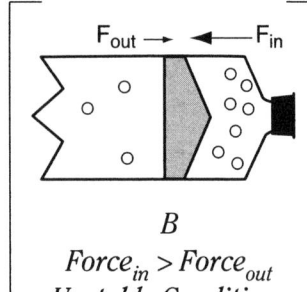
B
Force$_{in}$ > Force$_{out}$
Unstable Conditions

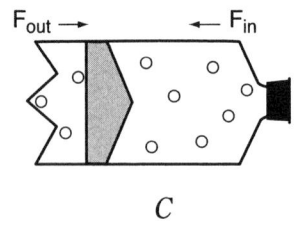
C
Equal Forces
Final Conditions

Teacher's Notes

Teacher Notes

10. *(Optional)* Look up the properties of high density PETE on the Internet. What characteristics of PETE make it an ideal plastic for use in soda bottles?

    PETE is an ideal plastic for soda bottles for several reasons. It is transparent, crystal clear, pure, tough, and unbreakable. PETE also has very low permeability to oxygen, carbon dioxide, and water, and excellent chemical resistance to acids and bases. If the PETE does not contain additives, it is relatively easy to recycle.

Supplementary Information

Construction of a Pressure Bottle

Cut off the top portion of a 2-L soda bottle. This will be used as a base or cap handle to hold the bottle caps that must be drilled. Screw one bottle cap securely onto the bottle top. Using a ½-inch drill and drill press, drill a hole through the center of the cap, as shown in Figure 5. (Notice you are drilling through the bottom of the cap.) Remove the cap from the bottle top, and use pliers to pull the valve stem through the hole from the inside, as shown below. The tire valve will stick out of the top of the bottle cap when it is placed on the soda bottle. Clear away any "chads" or spurs that may remain in the drilled hole. They will cause the seal to break.

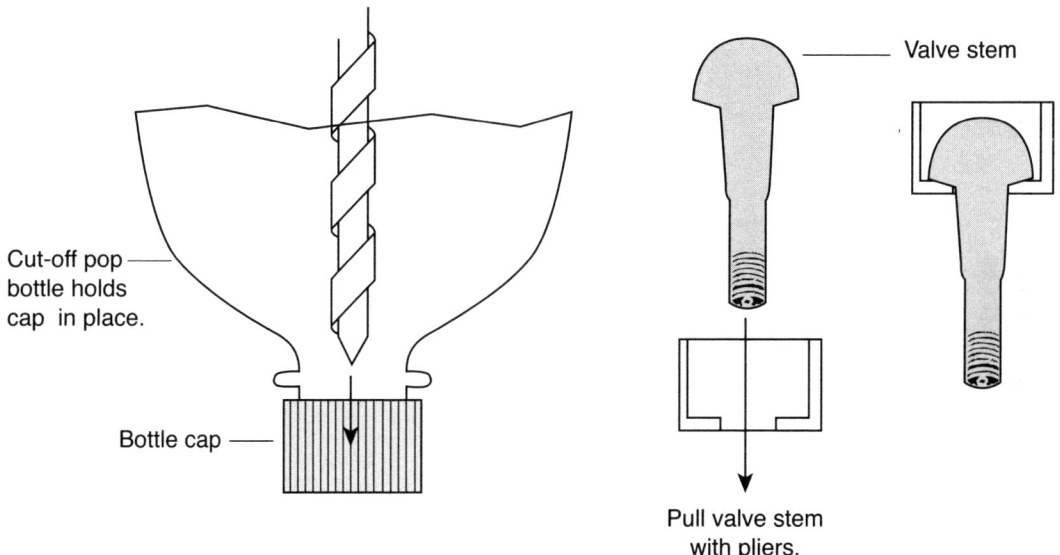

Figure 5.

If you are constructing home-made pressure bottles, it will be necessary to cut or saw off the flanges on the top of the syringes. Otherwise, the syringes will not fit inside the pressure bottles.

Teacher's Notes

Graphical Analysis and the Value of the Atmospheric Pressure

As observed in Post-Lab Question #6, the graph of total pressure versus 1/V is a straight line that passes through the origin (y-intercept equal to zero). This graph corresponds to an equation of the form $P_{total} = m \times 1/V$, where m is the slope of the line. If instead of the total pressure, students plot the gauge pressure ($P_{gauge} = P_{total} - P_{air}$) versus 1/V, they will obtain a straight line of the form $P_{gauge} = (m \times 1/V) - P_{air}$ (where the y-intercept is equal to $-P_{air}$). The value of P_{air} can be estimated by extending the best-fit straight line backwards to "negative" gauge pressures. The best estimate we were able to obtain using this method was about 12 psi (18% error).

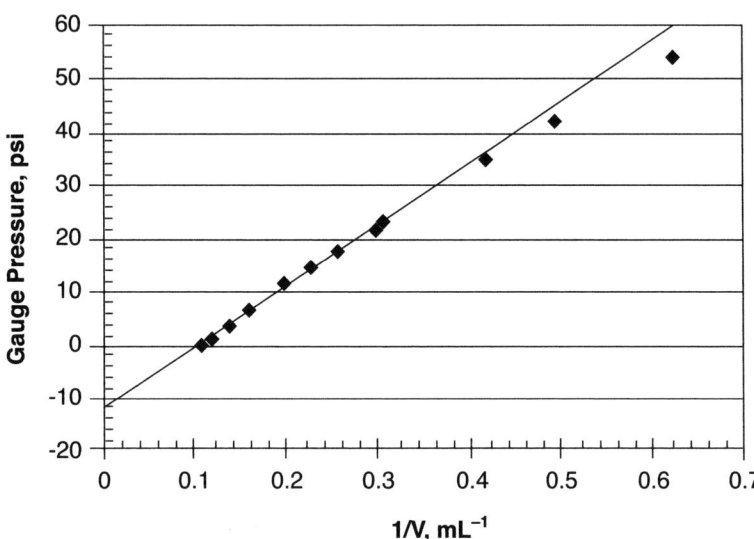

Algebraic Determination of the Value of the Atmospheric Pressure

It is also possibe to use the gauge pressure–volume measurements to estimate a value for the atmospheric pressure in psi. This is a nice algebraic challenge for students. According to Boyle's law, multiplying any two sets of P–V data should give the same result ($P_1V_1 = P_2V_2$). This is only true if the pressures are total pressures rather than relative gauge pressures ($P_{total} = P_{gauge} + x$, where x = value of atmospheric pressure in psi).

The following equation is obtained by combining the equations for Boyle's law and the total pressure:

$$(P_{gauge,\,1} + x)(V_1) = (P_{gauge,\,2} + x)(V_2)$$

Substituting the raw data for 17 psi and 1 psi (see *Sample Data* on page 11) into this equation gives:

$$(17 \text{ psi} + x)(3.8 \text{ mL}) = (1 \text{ psi} + x)(8.4 \text{ mL})$$

$$64.6 + 3.8x = 8.4 + 8.4x$$

$$56.2 = 4.6x$$

$$x = 12 \text{ psi}$$

The approaches shown here may be conceptually challenging for students but they lead to some interesting discussions. Are negative pressures possible? Why or why not?

Teacher Notes

Charles's Law and Absolute Zero
How Low Can You Go?

Introduction

Charles's law describes the relationship between the temperature of a gas and its volume. In order to understand this relationship, we must imagine what happens to the particles in a gas when it is heated or cooled. The temperature of a gas measures the average kinetic energy of the gas particles—how fast they are moving. When a gas is heated, the average kinetic energy of the particles increases and they move faster. When a gas is cooled, the average kinetic energy of the particles decreases and they move slower. Is there a lower limit to the temperature scale at which the particles stop moving altogether and their kinetic energy is zero? What would happen to the volume of a gas at this minimum temperature?

Concepts

- Temperature
- Absolute zero
- Charles's law
- Kinetic-molecular theory

Background

Applications of the gas laws are important in physiology, meteorology, scuba diving, even hot-air ballooning. Charles's law, which describes how the volume of a gas changes as it is heated or cooled, was inspired by one of these applications, the first sensational flight in the history of hot-air ballooning.

The world's first manned hot-air balloon flight took place in France in 1783. A few months later, Jacques Alexandre César Charles, professor of physics at the Sorbonne University in France, made the first flight in a lighter-than-air (hydrogen) balloon, climbing to a height of 9000 meters. Motivated by twin interests in science and ballooning, Charles not only made more flights, he also studied the factors that influence the flight of a hot air balloon. A hot air balloon works on the principle that the volume of a gas expands when heated. When the gas inside a balloon is heated, the gas expands and the hot air balloon becomes less dense than the air it displaces, causing the balloon to rise and float in the atmosphere.

Charles investigated this principle in the laboratory by measuring the increase in volume of a fixed amount of air when it was heated at a constant pressure. Charles's unpublished work was taken up by another French scientist and balloon enthusiast, Joseph-Louis Gay-Lussac, who studied the expansion of oxygen, hydrogen, nitrogen, carbon dioxide, nitrous oxide, and ammonia. In 1802 Gay-Lussac concluded that all of these gases expanded equally when heated from 0 to 100 °C—the volume of a gas is proportional to its temperature and does not depend on the nature of the gas.

This conclusion led to the development of more precise "air thermometers" for measuring temperature. Although very precise, air thermometers were still arbitrary—there was no absolute basis for any of the numbers on the scale. In 1848 the British mathematician William Thomson (knighted Lord Kelvin in 1866) proposed an absolute temperature scale based on the assumption that there must be a lower limit to temperature. He wrote:

*The volume of a gas is proportional to temperature. It is **directly** proportional only to the absolute temperature. Thus, in gas law calculations temperature must always be reported in kelvins.*

Charles's Law and Absolute Zero

Charles's Law and Absolute Zero – Page 2

> "... Infinite cold must correspond to a finite number of degrees of the air thermometer below zero, since if we push the strict principle of graduation ... sufficiently far, we should arrive at a point corresponding to the volume of air being reduced to nothing ..."

Thomson estimated a value for the "infinite cold" temperature on the Celsius scale. This temperature is known today as absolute zero and the temperature scale is called the Kelvin or *absolute temperature* scale. The units on this scale are equal in magnitude to the degree units on the Celsius scale and are called *kelvins* (abbreviated K), in honor of Lord Kelvin.

Experiment Overview

The purpose of this experiment is to carry out a modern version of classic experiments relating the volume and temperature of a gas. The experiment will be carried out using gases trapped inside sealed syringes. The syringes will be placed in water baths ranging in temperature from –15 °C to 80 °C. The volume of each gas will be measured at five different temperatures to test whether Charles's law is valid for different gases. The data will be plotted on a graph and then extrapolated backwards to estimate how low a temperature would be needed to reduce the volume of a gas to zero, that is, to reach absolute zero.

Pre-Lab Questions

Jacques Charles's original temperature–volume measurements were made using air trapped in a J-tube over mercury (Figure 1). When the tube was heated, the volume of the trapped air expanded. The volume of air was measured after the mercury level was adjusted so that the height of mercury was the same in the two ends of the tube.

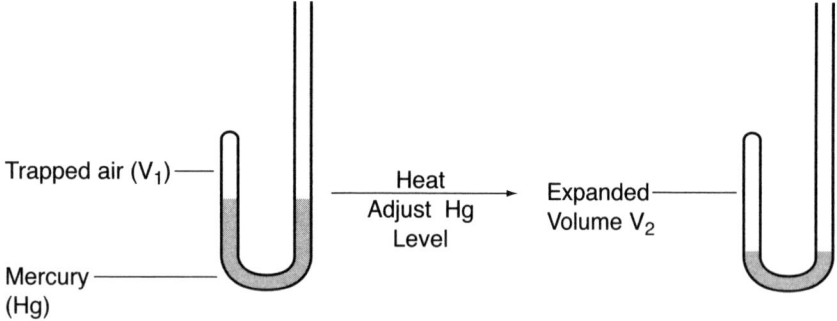

Figure 1.

1. What was the purpose of adjusting the mercury levels in the tube after it was heated? *Hint:* Recall how pressure can be measured using a mercury manometer.

2. According to our modern understanding of the gas laws, four physical properties (variables) are needed to describe the behavior of a gas. These variables are P (pressure), V (volume), T (temperature), and n (number of moles). In Charles's experiment, which two variables were held constant?

3. Fill in the blanks to summarize the relationship among the gas properties in Charles's experiment: For a fixed _____ of gas at constant _____, the _____ of a gas _____ as its _____ increases.

Teacher Notes

Charles's work was unpublished. Very little information is available on the details of how this experiment was actually performed. Gay-Lussac's translated and Thomson's original papers are available on the Internet and make very interesting reading. See the following Website for a collection of classic papers in the history of chemistry.

http://webserver.lemoyne.edu/faculty/giunta/papers.html

Page 3 – **Charles's Law and Absolute Zero**

Teacher Notes

Materials

Gas sources—air, hydrogen, helium, nitrogen, etc., 2
Silicone grease lubricant
Syringe, small, 10-mL
Syringe, large, 30-mL
Syringe tip caps, 2
Thermometer
Tongue depressor or wooden splint

Beakers, 400-mL, 5
Hot plate
Ice
Salt (sodium chloride)
Scoop spatula
Water

Safety Precautions

Handle pressurized gas sources (lecture bottles or gas cylinders) with caution. If working with hydrogen, avoid contact of the gas with any source of ignition (flames or sparks) in the lab. Wear gloves to apply silicone grease. Always wear chemical splash goggles whenever working with chemicals, glassware, or heat.

Procedure

1. Form a working group with three other students. The group should work together to obtain and share results for two different gases (Steps 4–10).

2. Obtain five 400-mL beakers and label them #1–5. Prepare water baths at different temperatures as follows:

   - Add crushed ice and a small amount of water (total volume 250 mL), followed by about 10 scoopfuls of salt, to beaker #1 to prepare a bath between –10 °C and –15 °C.
   - Add crushed ice and water to beaker #2 to prepare a bath at about 0 °C.
   - Add 250 mL of room temperature water to beaker #3 to prepare a 20 °C-bath.
   - Add 250 mL of hot running water to beaker #4 to prepare a 40–50 °C-bath.
   - Add 250 mL of water to beaker #5 and heat it on a hot plate at a medium setting to prepare a hot water bath at about 80 °C.

3. Add hot water or ice as needed during the course of the experiment to maintain the temperature of each bath within ±5 °C of the desired temperature.

4. Obtain one small and one large syringe. Lubricate the plunger of each syringe with silicone grease. Wearing gloves, apply a dab of grease to the black rubber gasket and use a wooden splint or tongue depressor to spread a thin layer of grease over the surface of the gasket.

5. Fill one syringe about ½-full with air and seal the syringe with a syringe tip cap.

6. Fill the second syringe with a different gas: Attach the syringe tip to a gas source, turn on the gas source, and pull on the plunger to fill the syringe completely with the gas. Disconnect the syringe from the gas source, push on the syringe to expel the gas, then reattach the syringe to the gas source and fill the syringe about ½-full again. Seal the syringe with a syringe tip cap and record the identity of the gas (hydrogen, helium, etc.).

The exact temperatures of the water baths are not important as long as students measure volumes over a wide enough temperature range. The difference in temperature between any two baths should be at least 15–20 °C.

Charles's Law and Absolute Zero

Charles's Law and Absolute Zero – Page 4

Teacher Notes

7. Place the first syringe in the coldest water bath (beaker #1) and submerge the syringe just up to the bottom of the plunger (Figure 2). Hold it there for 3–4 minutes, then quickly push down on the plunger once and release it. Measure and record the temperature of the water bath.

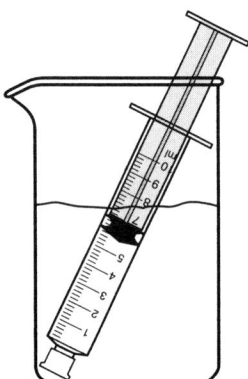

Figure 2.

8. Measure and record the volume when the plunger stops moving. *Note:* Keep the syringe in the water bath the entire time.

9. Remove the syringe from the first bath and place it in the second temperature bath. After two minutes, measure the new temperature and volume of the gas.

10. Repeat step 9 in the remaining water baths to obtain a total of five different temperature–volume readings.

11. Repeat steps 7–10 with the second syringe filled with a different gas.

Teacher Notes

Name: _____

Class/Lab Period: _____

Charles's Law and Absolute Zero

Data and Results Table

10-mL Syringe		30-mL Syringe	
Identity of Gas		**Identity of Gas**	
Temperature	**Volume**	**Temperature**	**Volume**

Post-Lab Questions *(Use a separate sheet of paper to answer questions 2–7.)*

1. Plot the data obtained for each gas on the following graph. Use the left-hand y-axis for the small syringe, the right-hand y-axis for the large syringe. Scale each axis as needed.

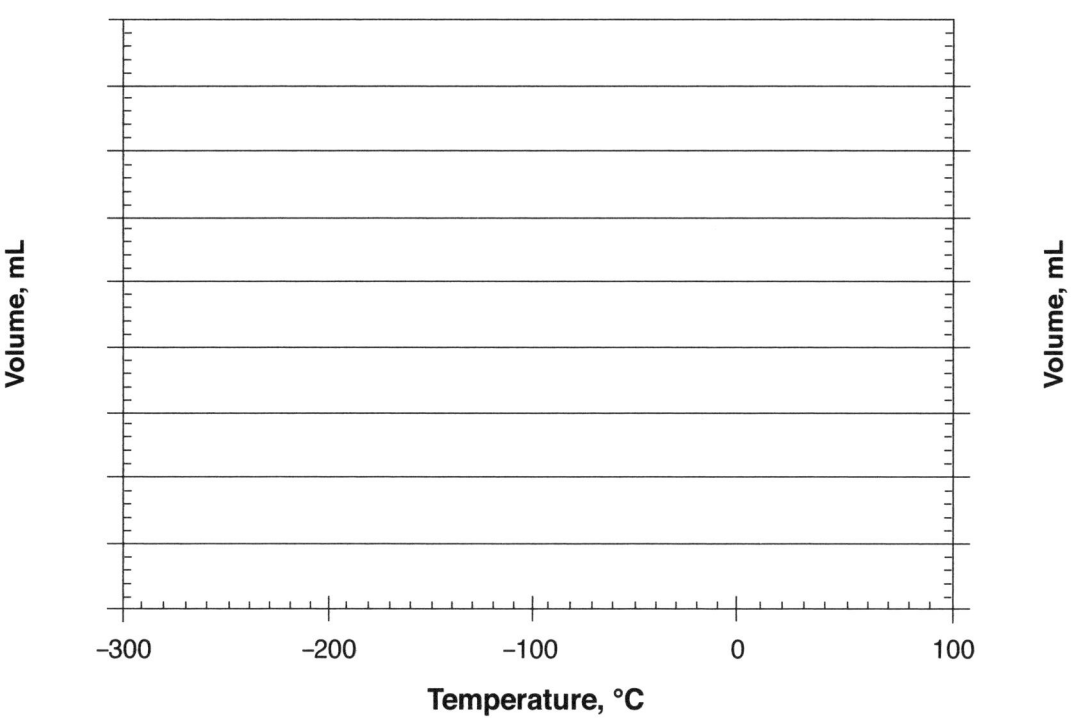

Charles's Law and Absolute Zero – Page 6

Teacher Notes

2. Using a straight-edge, draw a best-fit straight line through the volume–temperature data points for each gas. Is the volume of a gas proportional to its temperature over the entire temperature range studied?

3. For each gas, extend (extrapolate) the straight line backwards to estimate the minimum (Kelvin's "infinite cold") temperature that would be needed to reduce the volume of the gas to zero. Average the two points to determine the value of absolute zero.

4. What is the accepted (literature) value for absolute zero? How close to this value is your estimate of absolute zero? The estimate is very sensitive to the slope of the line through the data points. Why?

5. Charles's law describes how gases behave when heated, but does not explain why. Our best model for explaining the behavior of gases is called the kinetic-molecular theory (KMT). According to this model, the average kinetic energy of a gas depends on the temperature. Pressure, defined as force per unit area, results from the collision of gas particles with the walls of the container. Use the KMT to explain how and why the volume of a gas in a *flexible* container (such as a syringe or a balloon) will change when the gas is heated.

6. According to the KMT, the volume of the gas particles is extremely small compared to the volume the gas occupies—most of the volume of gas is "empty space." Based on your results, does Charles's law depend on the identity of the gas? On the amount (mass) of the gas? Explain in terms of the KMT and the amount of empty space in a gas.

7. Predict how each of the following properties of an ideal gas will change as a gas is cooled to near absolute zero in a flexible container:

Average velocity of gas particles	
Spacing between gas particles	
Pressure exerted by gas particles	
Mass of the particles	
Volume of the gas	
Density of the gas	
Attractive forces between gas particles	

8. *(Optional)* In their quest to reach absolute zero, scientists have come very, very close, but have never reached true absolute zero. Why is it *theoretically* impossible to reach absolute zero?

Teacher Notes

Teacher's Notes
Charles's Law and Absolute Zero

Master Materials List *(for a class of 28 students working in groups of four)*

Gas sources—air, hydrogen, helium, nitrogen, etc.*	Beakers, 400-mL, 35
Silicone grease lubricant	Hot plates, 5†
Syringes, small, 10-mL, 7	Ice, 4 liters
Syringes, large, 30-mL, 7	Salt (sodium chloride), 300 g
Syringe tip caps, 14	Scoop spatulas, 7
Thermometers, 7	Water
Tongue depressors or wooden splints, 15	

*See the Sample Data and Lab Hints sections for suggestions.
†Several student groups may share hot plates and hot water baths.

Safety Precautions

Handle pressurized gas sources (lecture bottles or gas cylinders) with caution. If working with hydrogen, avoid contact of the gas with any source of ignition (flames or sparkers) in the lab. Wear gloves to apply silicone grease. Always wear chemical splash goggles whenever working with chemicals, glassware, or heat. Please consult current Material Safety Data Sheets for any gases used in this experiment.

Disposal

The syringes should be taken apart and wiped clean with a paper towel to remove the silicone grease. Wash the syringes with mild, soapy water and store the syringes for future use.

Lab Hints

- The laboratory work for this experiment can reasonably be completed within a normal 50-minute class period. Teachers who have access to computer-based graphing programs (such as Vernier's Graphical Analysis 3.0 Software, see Flinn Catalog No. TC1404) may want to schedule additional time for students to graph and analyze their data. The graphs will be more precise than hand-drawn graphs and will allow students to obtain more accurate estimates of absolute zero.

- Silicone grease was found to be the most effective syringe lubricant for the different gases across the temperature range recommended in this experiment. Although petroleum jelly worked well with an air-filled syringe, it could not be used with other gases, including hydrogen, helium, and nitrogen, at temperatures above about 50 °C (the plunger would get stuck).

- Five temperature points are recommended in the *Procedure* section. Adding a below zero water bath (–15 °C) gave a more accurate estimate of absolute zero than adding a boiling water bath.

Teacher's Notes

- The procedure was tested for five different gases (air, nitrogen, hydrogen, helium, and carbon dioxide) in three different size syringes (10-, 30-, and 60-mL) in order to test the reliability and reproducibility of the method. Refer to the *Supplementary Information* on page 30 for additional sample graphs. The results were remarkably consistent for different gases and different sample sizes. The *Sample Data* on page 26 summarize the results obtained with air and hydrogen in 10- and 30-mL syringes. Since the most accurate results were obtained with 10- and 30-mL syringe sizes, the 60-mL syringes are not recommended in the *Materials* section. Teachers who have 60-mL syringes may want to include them in this experiment for comparison. A good question for students then would be why the results are less reliable in larger syringes (it takes longer to cool or heat the gas in a larger syringe and the syringe volumes are less precise). Smaller syringes (e.g., 5 mL) do not give sufficient volume changes.

- It is not necessary to test different gases in order to verify Charles's law and determine absolute zero in this experiment. However, using different gases shows that the ideal gas behavior implied by the gas laws also describes "real" gases under a variety of conditions. By making available a variety of gases for different student groups to test, teachers can encourage a more collaborative learning environment.

- Gases are available in convenient lecture bottle and refillable cylinder sizes. Consult your current *Flinn Scientific Catalog/Reference Manual* for a complete listing of gas sources and supplies, including regulator valves. Be creative and flexible in locating alternative gas sources for this experiment. Helium-filled Mylar™ balloons, for instance, are inexpensive sources of helium. Gas outlets in the lab may be used as sources of methane (natural gas). Fill the syringes ahead of time in the hood and seal them prior to dispensing them to the students. Exercise caution when working with natural gas to prevent accidental exposure to flames or other sources of ignition. Gases may also be generated in the lab using a homemade gas-delivery apparatus. Call or write us at Flinn Scientific to obtain a complimentary copy of our ChemFax Publication #10527, "Construction of a Simple Gas Delivery Method."

Teaching Tips

- As mentioned in the *Background* section, both Jacques Charles and Joseph Gay-Lussac were at least partially inspired by their interests in hot-air ballooning to study the properties of gases. If it worked for them, it may work for your students as well! Inspire your students to learn more about the properties of gases with the hot-air balloon activity kit "Up, Up, and Away" (Flinn Catalog No. AP6310). The kit contains enough materials for 15 pairs of students to construct and launch their own giant hot-air balloon. Students will learn how hot-air balloons lift from the ground, stay afloat, and eventually descend.

- Why did it take more than 40 years to go from Charles's law (Gay-Lussac's Law in Europe) to a definition and value for absolute zero? The answer has to do with the lack of a functional definition of heat in the early 19th century. Thomson's groundbreaking paper on the value of absolute zero followed immediately upon Joule's famous experiment demonstrating the mechanical equivalent of heat energy. Thomson estimated the value of absolute zero based on the coefficient of expansion of gases (the relative increase in the volume of a gas per degree Celsius).

Teacher's Notes

Teacher Notes

Answers to Pre-Lab Questions *(Student answers will vary.)*

Jacques Charles's original temperature–volume measurements were made using air trapped in a J-tube over mercury (Figure 1). When the tube was heated, the volume of the trapped air expanded. The volume of air was measured after the mercury level was adjusted so that the height of mercury was equal in the two ends of the tube.

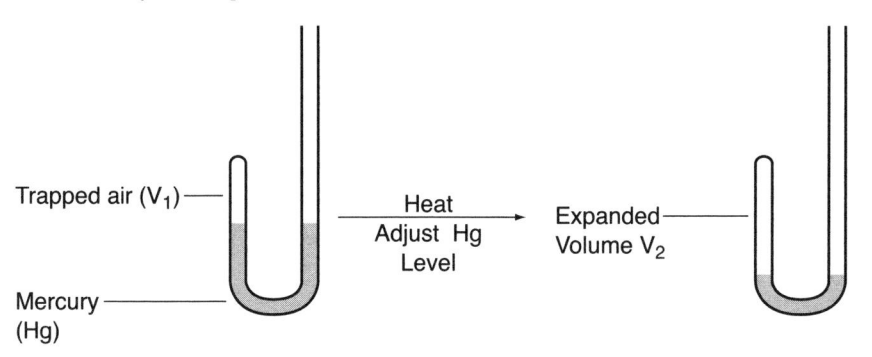

Trapped air (V_1) — Heat, Adjust Hg Level → Expanded Volume V_2

Mercury (Hg)

Figure 1.

1. What was the purpose of adjusting the mercury level in the tube after it was heated? *Hint: Recall how pressure can be measured using a mercury manometer.*

   When a gas is heated, both the volume and pressure of the gas will tend to increase. Charles's original experiment was designed to test the expansion of a gas at a constant pressure equal to that of the surrounding air. Adjusting the mercury level in the two ends of the tube permitted Charles to equalize the pressure of the trapped air sample with that of the surrounding air (atmospheric pressure).

2. According to our modern understanding of the gas laws, four physical properties (variables) are needed to describe the behavior of a gas. These variables are P (pressure), V (volume), T (temperature), and n (number of moles). In Charles's experiment, which two variables were held constant?

   Both the pressure (P) and the number of moles of gas (n) were held constant in Charles's experiment.

3. Fill in the blanks to summarize the relationship among the gas properties in Charles's experiments:

   *For a fixed **number of moles** of gas at constant **pressure**, the **volume** of a gas **increases** as its **temperature** increases.*

Sample Data

Student data will vary.

Data and Results Table*

10-mL Syringe		10-mL Syringe	
Identity of Gas	Air	**Identity of Gas**	Hydrogen
Temperature (°C)	**Volume (mL)**	**Temperature (°C)**	**Volume (mL)**
–15	4.4	–14	4.3
0	4.6	0	4.5
21	5.0	21	4.8
48	5.4	52	5.4
80	5.9	80	5.8

30-mL Syringe		30-mL Syringe	
Identity of Gas	Air	**Identity of Gas**	Hydrogen
Temperature (°C)	**Volume (mL)**	**Temperature (°C)**	**Volume (mL)**
–14	13.6	–14	12.5
0	14.1	1	13.0
20	15.1	21	14.0
40	16.0	52	15.5
71	18.1	80	17.0

*Each working group of four students is only responsible for two trials. Sample data are presented for a total of four trials, two different gases in two different size syringes, in order to demonstrate the range of results that might be expected in a classroom setting. See the *Supplementary Information* section for results with other gases in other size syringes.

Teacher's Notes

Teacher Notes

Answers to Post-Lab Questions *(Student answers will vary.)*

1. Plot the data obtained for each gas on the following graph. Use the left-hand y-axis for the small syringe, the right-hand y-axis for the large syringe. Scale each axis as needed.

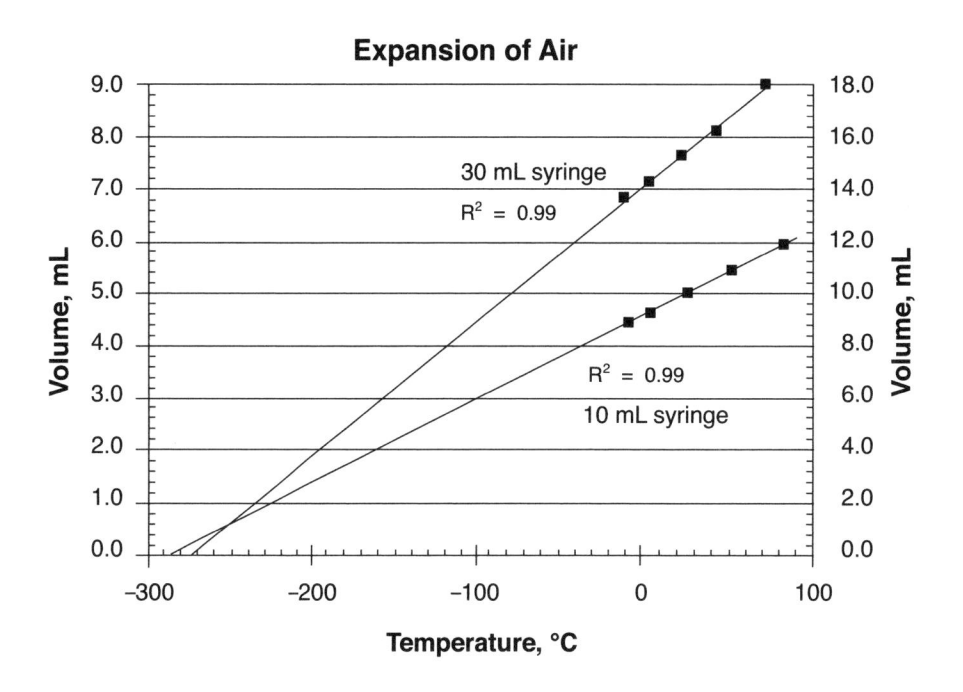

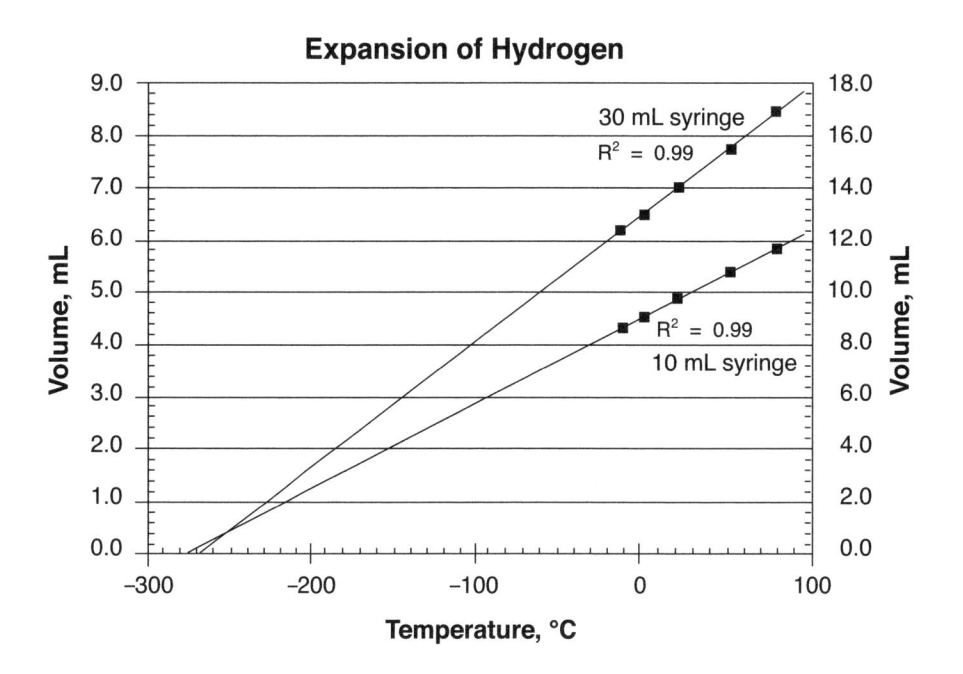

Expansion of Air

Expansion of Hydrogen

2. Using a straight-edge, draw a best-fit straight line through the volume–temperature data points for each gas. Is the volume of a gas proportional to its temperature over the entire temperature range studied?

   It appears that for each sample all of the volume–temperature data points fall on a straight line. This means that the volume of a gas is proportional to temperature.

Teacher's Notes

See the Sample Graphs for the best-fit straight lines through the data. **Note to teachers:** *Very small changes in the best-fit straight line as it passes through the data points lead to very large changes in where the line crosses the x-axis. This means that students who know what the value of absolute zero should be can easily "cheat" by drawing a best-fit straight line that gives this exact value of absolute zero! The lines in the Sample Graphs were obtained by linear regression.*

3. For each gas, extend (extrapolate) the straight line backwards to estimate the minimum (Kelvin's "infinite cold") temperature that would be needed to reduce the volume of the gas to zero. Average the two points to determine the value of absolute zero.

    The following values of absolute zero were extrapolated from the Sample Graphs.

    For air, 10-mL syringe: –285 °C.
    For air, 30-mL syringe: –274 °C.
    For hydrogen, 10-mL syringe, –275 °C.
    For hydrogen, 30-mL syringe, –267 °C.
    Average value of absolute zero: –275 °C.

4. What is the accepted (literature) value for absolute zero? How close to this value is your estimate of absolute zero? The estimate is very sensitive to the slope of the line through the data points. Why?

    The literature value for absolute zero is –273.15 °C. The estimate of absolute zero from the graphs is very close to its actual value. The estimated value of absolute zero changes significantly if the slope of the line through the data points changes even slightly. This is because the data points are so far away (260 °C) from the extrapolated value we are looking for.

5. Charles's law describes how gases behave when heated, but does not explain why. Our best model for explaining the behavior of gases is called the kinetic-molecular theory (KMT). According to this model, the average kinetic energy of a gas depends only on the temperature. Pressure, defined as force per unit area, results from the collision of gas particles with the walls of the container. Use the KMT to explain how and why the volume of a gas in a flexible container (such as a syringe or a balloon) will change when the gas is heated.

    When a gas is heated in a flexible or elastic container, the volume will tend to expand so that the pressure inside the container is the same as the pressure of the surrounding air outside the container. As a gas is heated, the average kinetic energy of the gas particles increases and the particles move faster. As the particles move faster in the same size container, they will collide more often and with more force against the inside walls of the container. If the walls of the container are flexible, this additional force pushes out or expands the container.

6. According to the KMT, the volume of the gas particles is extremely small compared to the volume the gas occupies—most of the volume of a gas is "empty space." Based on your results, does Charles's law depend on the identity of the gas? On the amount (mass) of the gas? Explain in terms of the KMT and the amount of empty space in a gas.

Teacher's Notes

Teacher Notes

The relationship between the volume of a gas and its temperature was found to be the same both for different gases and for different size samples. This means that Charles's law is independent of the identity of a gas and the number of moles of gas. This makes sense in terms of the KMT—since most of the volume of a gas is empty space, the relative size (molecular weight or volume) of a gas particle does not have an appreciable effect on the overall volume of the gas sample.

7. Predict how each of the following properties of an ideal gas will change as a gas is cooled to near absolute zero in a flexible container:

Average velocity of gas particles	*Will decrease until at absolute zero the average velocity is zero.*
Spacing between gas particles	*Will decrease until at absolute zero there is no spacing between the gas particles.*
Pressure exerted by gas particles	*Will decrease as velocity and force of collisions decrease.*
Mass of the particles	*Does not change.*
Volume of the gas	*Will decrease until at absolute zero the volume should be zero. This is theoretically impossible.*
Density of the gas	*Will increase as the volume decreases and approaches infinity at absolute zero.*
Attractive forces between gas particles	*In the ideal gas model there are no attractive forces. For real gases the forces between particles will increase as they get closer together.*

8. *(Optional)* In their quest to reach absolute zero, scientists have come very, very close, but have never reached true absolute zero. Why is it *theoretically* impossible to reach absolute zero?

   Note to teachers: *This is a difficult question! On a basic level, we define matter as having mass and occupying space—the volume cannot be zero, and so the temperature cannot be zero. A more compelling argument is that in order to cool something, heat must flow out of a system at higher temperature to one at lower temperature. Since there cannot be a reservoir below absolute zero, heat cannot flow out of a system to reach absolute zero. Physicists argue that absolute zero is impossible because the third law of thermodynamics says so and because it violates the principles of quantum mechanics.*

The quest for absolute zero has proved rewarding for scientists. In 1997 Steven Chu, William Phillips, and Claude Cohen-Tannoudji shared the Nobel Prize in Physics for their development of methods to cool atoms to 1×10^{-5} K by trapping atoms in a laser beam. In 2001 Eric Cornell, Wolfgang Ketterle, and Carl Wieman shared the Nobel Prize in Physics for their discovery of a new state of matter at 2×10^{-9} K. The new state of matter is called the Bose–Einstein condensate.

Teacher's Notes

Supplementary Information

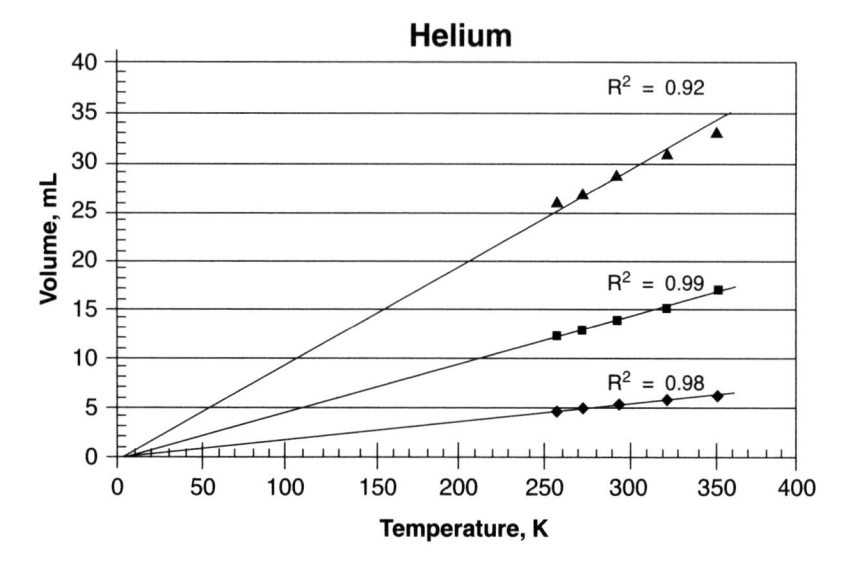

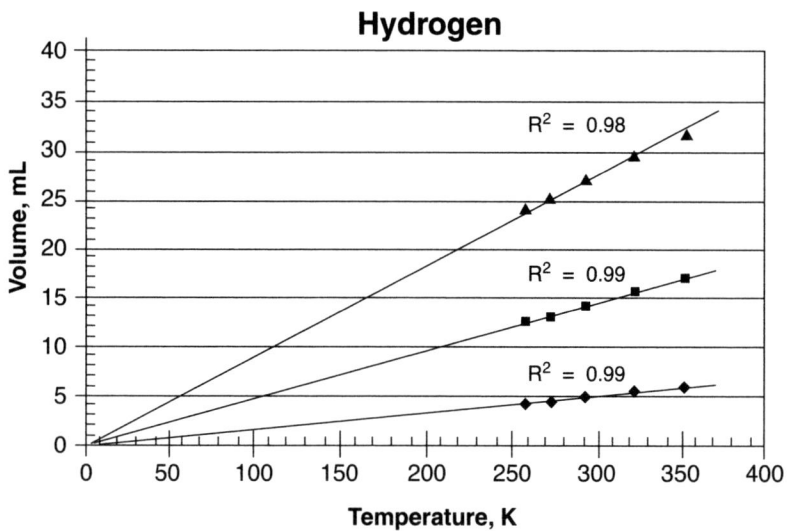

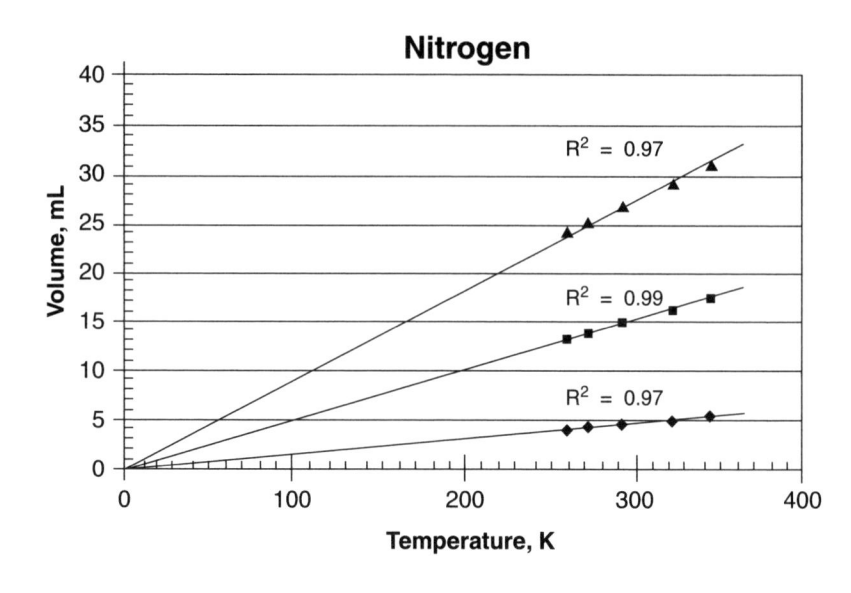

Helium

Hydrogen

Nitrogen

The sample graphs on this page were obtained for three different gases using three different size syringes (10-, 30-, and 60-mL). All of the lines were drawn to pass through the origin. The R^2 values show the excellent correlation with absolute zero.

Teacher Notes

Molar Volume of Hydrogen
Combining the Gas Laws

Introduction

Airbags have been required safety features on new cars since the 1980s and are credited with saving thousands of lives over that time. Airbags contain a compound that decomposes to give nitrogen gas upon impact from a collision. How much nitrogen gas must be generated to fill an airbag? The amount of gas needed to fill any size container can be calculated if we know the molar volume of the gas.

Concepts

- Avogadro's law
- Ideal gas law
- Dalton's law
- Molar volume

Background

Avogadro's law states that equal volumes of gases contain equal numbers of molecules under the same conditions of temperature and pressure. It follows, therefore, that all gas samples containing the same number of molecules will occupy the same volume if the temperature and pressure are kept constant. The volume occupied by one mole of a gas is called the *molar volume*. In this experiment we will measure the molar volume of hydrogen gas at standard temperature and pressure (STP, equal to 273 K and 1 atm).

The reaction of magnesium metal with hydrochloric acid (Equation 1) provides a convenient means of generating small-scale quantities of hydrogen in the lab.

$$Mg(s) + 2HCl(aq) \rightarrow MgCl_2(aq) + H_2(g) \qquad \textit{Equation 1}$$

If the reaction is carried out with excess hydrochloric acid, the volume of hydrogen gas obtained will depend on the number of moles of magnesium as well as on the pressure and temperature. The molar volume of hydrogen can be calculated if we measure the volume occupied by a sample containing a known number of moles of hydrogen. Since the volume will be measured under laboratory conditions of temperature and pressure, the measured volume must be corrected to STP conditions before calculating the molar volume.

The relationship among the four gas variables—pressure (P), volume (V), temperature (T), and the number of moles (n)—is expressed in the ideal gas law (Equation 2), where R is a constant called the universal gas constant.

$$PV = nRT \qquad \textit{Equation 2}$$

The ideal gas law reduces to Equation 3, the combined gas law, if the number of moles of gas is constant. The combined gas law can be used to calculate the volume (V_2) of a gas at STP (T_2 and P_2) from the volume (V_1) measured under any other set of laboratory conditions (T_1 and P_1). In using either the ideal gas law or the combined gas law, remember that temperature must be always be expressed in units of kelvins (K) on the absolute temperature scale.

Molar Volume of Hydrogen – Page 2

$$\frac{P_1V_1}{T_1} = \frac{P_2V_2}{T_2} \qquad \text{Equation 3}$$

Hydrogen gas will be collected by the displacement of water in an inverted graduated cylinder using the apparatus shown in Figure 1. The total pressure of the gas in the cylinder will be equal to the barometric (air) pressure. However, the gas in the cylinder will not be pure hydrogen. The gas will also contain water vapor due to the evaporation of the water molecules over which it is being collected. According to Dalton's law, the total pressure of the gas will be equal to the partial pressure of hydrogen plus the partial pressure of water vapor (Equation 4). The vapor pressure of water depends only on the temperature (see Table 1).

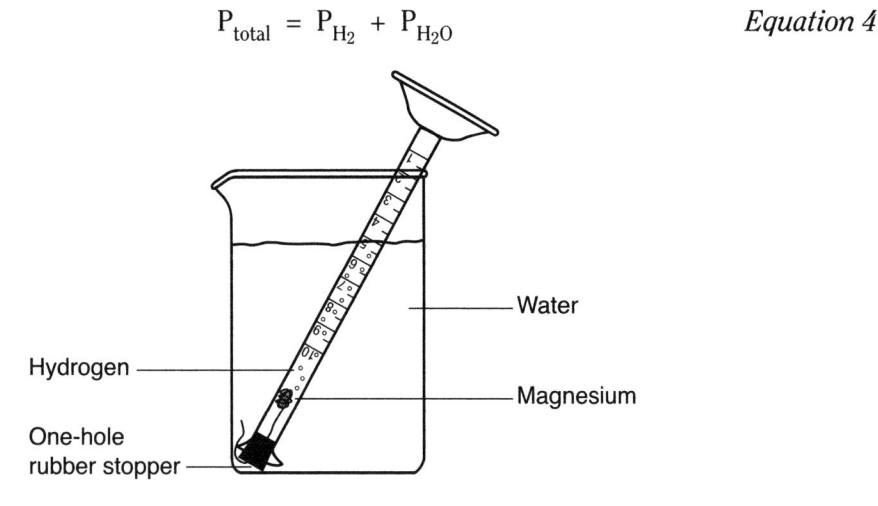

$$P_{total} = P_{H_2} + P_{H_2O} \qquad \text{Equation 4}$$

Figure 1.

Table 1. Vapor Pressure of Water at Different Temperatures

Temperature, °C	P_{H_2O}, mm Hg	Temperature, °C	P_{H_2O}, mm Hg
16 °C	13.6	22 °C	19.8
17 °C	14.5	23 °C	21.1
18 °C	15.5	24 °C	22.4
19 °C	16.5	25 °C	23.8
20 °C	17.5	26 °C	25.2
21 °C	18.7	27 °C	26.7

Experiment Overview

The purpose of this experiment is to determine the volume of one mole of hydrogen gas at standard temperature and pressure (STP). Hydrogen will be generated by the reaction of a known mass of magnesium with excess hydrochloric acid in an inverted graduated cylinder filled with water. The volume of hydrogen collected by water displacement will be measured and corrected for differences in temperature and pressure in order to calculate the molar volume of hydrogen at STP.

Teacher Notes

Pre-Lab Questions

Reaction of 0.028 g of magnesium with excess hydrochloric acid generated 31.0 mL of hydrogen gas. The gas was collected by water displacement in a water bath 22 °C. The barometric pressure in the lab that day was 746 mm Hg.

1. Use Dalton's law and the vapor pressure of water at 22 °C (Table 1) to calculate the partial pressure of hydrogen gas in the gas collecting tube.

2. Use the combined gas law to calculate the "corrected" volume of hydrogen at STP. *Hint:* Watch your units for temperature and pressure!

3. What is the theoretical number of moles of hydrogen that can be produced from 0.028 g of Mg? *Hint:* Refer to Equation 1 for the balanced equation for the reaction.

4. Divide the corrected volume of hydrogen by the theoretical number of moles of hydrogen to calculate the molar volume (in 4 mol) of hydrogen at STP.

Materials

Copper wire, Cu, 18-gauge, 10-cm long
Hydrochloric acid, HCl, 2 M, 10 mL
Magnesium ribbon, Mg, 1-cm pieces, 2
Distilled or deionized water
Wash bottle
Barometer

Beaker, 400-mL
Graduated cylinder, 10-mL
Metric ruler
One-hole rubber stopper, size 1 or 2
Scissors or wire cutter
Thermometer

Safety Precautions

Hydrochloric acid is a corrosive liquid. Avoid contact with eyes and skin and clean up all spills immediately. Magnesium metal is a flammable solid. Keep away from flames and other sources of ignition. Wear chemical splash goggles and chemical-resistant gloves and apron. Wash hands thoroughly with soap and water before leaving the laboratory.

Procedure

1. Fill a 400-mL beaker about ¾-full with water.

2. Obtain or cut a 1-cm piece of magnesium ribbon. Measure and record the exact length of the magnesium ribbon to the nearest 0.1 cm. Do not exceed 1.0 cm.

3. Your teacher will provide a conversion factor in g/cm to calculate the mass of magnesium used in this experiment. Multiply the length of magnesium ribbon by this conversion factor to calculate the mass of the 1-cm piece of magnesium obtained in step 2. Record the mass of magnesium in the data table.

4. Obtain a piece of copper wire about 10-cm long. Twist and fold one end of the copper wire around a pencil to make a small "cage" into which the magnesium ribbon may be inserted. See Figure 2.

5. Firmly place the 1-cm piece of magnesium into the copper-wire cage.

Figure 2.

To get students to measure the magnesium strip more carefully, ask them to measure the length across both the top and bottom sides and average them. This may also help students obtain "square" cuts. There is little room for error when the gas is collected in a 10-mL graduated cylinder. Paying attention to detail will help!

Molar Volume of Hydrogen – Page 4

6. Insert the straight end of the copper wire into a one-hole rubber stopper so that the cage end containing the magnesium is about 1-cm below the bottom of the stopper (see Figure 1). Hook the end of the copper wire around the top of the stopper to hold the cage in place.

7. Obtain about 5 mL of 2 M hydrochloric acid in a tall-form, 10-mL graduated cylinder.

8. While holding the graduated cylinder in a tipped position, slowly and carefully fill the graduated cylinder with distilled water from a wash bottle or a plastic pipet. Work slowly to avoid mixing the acid and water layers at this time. Fill the graduated cylinder all the way to the top so that no air remains in the cylinder.

9. Insert the magnesium–copper wire–stopper assembly into the graduated cylinder. The magnesium piece should be above the 10-mL line on the graduated cylinder (see Figure 1).

10. Place your finger over the hole of the rubber stopper, invert the graduated cylinder, and carefully lower the stoppered end of the graduated cylinder into the 400-mL beaker containing water.

11. Record any evidence of a chemical reaction in the data table.

12. If the magnesium metal "escapes" its copper cage, gently shake the graduated cylinder up and down to work it back into the acidic solution.

13. Allow the apparatus to stand for 5 minutes after the magnesium has completely reacted. Gently tap the sides of the graduated cylinder to dislodge any gas bubbles that may have become attached to the sides.

14. Gently move the graduated cylinder up or down in the water bath until the water level inside the graduated cylinder is the same as the water level in the beaker. This is done to equalize the pressure with the surrounding air (barometric pressure). *Note:* Be careful to make sure that the stoppered end of the graduated cylinder remains submerged in the water.

15. When the water levels inside and outside the cylinder are the same, measure and record the exact volume of hydrogen gas in the graduated cylinder.

16. Since the cylinder is upside down in the water bath, the volume reading obtained in step 14 must be corrected for the fact that the meniscus was read upside down as well. Subtract 0.2 mL from the volume recorded in step 15 and record the "corrected" volume of hydrogen gas in the data table.

17. Measure and record the temperature of the water bath in the beaker. Using a barometer, measure and record the barometric pressure in the lab.

18. Remove the graduated cylinder from the water bath and discard the water in the beaker as directed by your instructor.

19. Repeat the entire procedure to obtain a second set of data. Record this as Trial 2 in the data table. If time permits, perform a third trial as well.

Teacher Notes

If the barometric pressure in your area is low (due to elevation or a thunderstorm), carry out this reaction in a water bath at 0–5 °C rather than at room temperature. See the Lab Hints *section for more information.*

Teacher Notes

Name: _____

Class/Lab Period: _____

Molar Volume of Hydrogen

Data Table

	Trial 1	Trial 2
Length of Mg Ribbon		
Mass of Mg		
Evidence of Chemical Reaction		
Volume of H_2 Gas		
Corrected Volume of H_2		
Temperature of Water Bath		
Barometric Pressure		

Post-Lab Calculations and Analysis

Construct a Results Table to summarize the results of the following calculations.

1. Calculate the theoretical number of moles of hydrogen gas produced in Trials 1 and 2.

2. Use Table 1 in the *Background* section to find the vapor pressure of water at the temperature of the water bath in this experiment. Calculate the partial pressure of hydrogen gas produced in Trials 1 and 2.

3. Use the combined gas law to convert the measured volume of hydrogen to the volume the gas would occupy at STP for Trials 1 and 2. *Hint:* Remember the units!

4. Divide the volume of hydrogen gas at STP by the theoretical number of moles of hydrogen to calculate the molar volume of hydrogen for Trials 1 and 2.

Teachers must measure the linear density of the magnesium ribbon and provide this information to students. Measure the exact length of a 50- or 100-cm piece of magnesium ribbon and obtain its mass to two decimal places. Divide the mass in grams by the length in centimeters to obtain the linear density conversion factor (g/cm).

Molar Volume of Hydrogen

Molar Volume of Hydrogen – *Page 6*

5. What is the average value of the molar volume of hydrogen? Look up the literature value of the molar volume of a gas in your textbook and calculate the percent error in your experimental determination of the molar volume of hydrogen.

$$\text{Percent error} = \frac{|\text{Experimental value} - \text{Literature value}|}{\text{Literature value}} \times 100\%$$

6. One mole of hydrogen gas has a mass of 2.02 g. Use your value of the molar volume of hydrogen to calculate the mass of one liter of hydrogen gas at STP. This is the density of hydrogen in g/L. How does this experimental value of the density compare with the literature value? (Consult a chemistry handbook for the density of hydrogen.)

7. In setting up this experiment, a student noticed that a bubble of air leaked into the graduated cylinder when it was inverted in the water bath. What effect would this have on the measured volume of hydrogen gas? Would the calculated molar volume of hydrogen be too high or too low as a result of this error? Explain.

8. A student noticed that the magnesium ribbon appeared to be oxidized—the metal surface was black and dull rather than silver and shiny. What effect would this error have on the measured volume of hydrogen gas? Would the calculated molar volume of hydrogen be too high or too low as a result of this error? Explain.

9. *(Optional)* Your teacher wants to scale up this experiment for demonstration purposes and would like to collect the gas in an inverted 50-mL buret. Use the ideal gas law to calculate the maximum length of magnesium ribbon that your teacher should use.

Teacher Notes

The demonstration suggested in Question #9 will work. Since the scale markings do not start at the bottom of the buret, however, you will have to open the stopcock to let in some air before beginning the demo. Let in just enough air to reduce the water level to the 50.0-mL mark. Measure the difference in volume to determine the volume of gas collected in the demonstration.

Teacher's Notes
Molar Volume of Hydrogen

Master Materials List *(for a class of 30 students working in pairs)*

Copper wire, Cu, 16- to 20-gauge, 1.5 m	Beakers, 400-mL, 15
Hydrochloric acid, HCl, 2 M, 150 mL	Graduated cylinders, 10-mL, 15
Magnesium ribbon, Mg, 1-cm pieces, 30	Metric rulers, 15
Distilled or deionized water	One-hole rubber stoppers, size 1 or 2, 15
Wash bottles, 15	Scissors or wire cutters, 5–7
Barometer (optional)	Thermometers, 15

Preparation of Solutions

Hydrochloric Acid, 2 M: Place about 250 mL of distilled or deionized water in a flask and add 83 mL of 12 M hydrochloric acid. Stir to mix and then dilute to 500 mL. *Note:* Always add acid to water.

Safety Precautions

Hydrochloric acid is a corrosive liquid. Avoid contact with eyes and skin and clean up all spills immediately. Magnesium metal is a flammable solid. Keep away from flames and other sources of ignition. Wear chemical splash goggles and chemical-resistant gloves and apron. Wash hands thoroughly with soap and water before leaving the laboratory. Please consult current Material Safety Data Sheets for additional safety, handling, and disposal information.

Disposal

Please consult your current *Flinn Scientific Catalog/Reference Manual* for general guidelines and specific procedures governing the disposal of laboratory waste. The water bath solutions remaining after the hydrogen gas has been collected will be acidic. These should be neutralized with base (sodium bicarbonate is a good choice) and flushed down the drain with excess water according to Flinn Suggested Disposal Method #24b.

Students should participate in the disposal process by neutralizing the acidic waste solutions prior to rinsing them down the drain. As an additional pre-lab question or for extra credit, ask students to calculate the mass of sodium bicarbonate required to neutralize the initial amount of HCl.

Lab Hints

- The laboratory work for this experiment can reasonably be completed within a normal 50-minute class period. The reaction of magnesium with hydrochloric acid on the microscale level recommended in this experiment takes about five minutes to proceed to completion. This allows students the opportunity to work through the procedure and conduct two or more runs in a typical lab period. The *PreLab Questions* may be assigned as homework in preparation for lab or may be used as part of a cooperative classroom discussion. Doing the prelab will help students understand the calculations needed to complete their lab report.

- The amount of hydrogen generated depends on the length of magnesium ribbon used, its linear density (mass in grams per centimeter), and the purity (freshness) of the metal. The linear density, in turn, depends on the thickness of the metal ribbon and will typically vary between 0.0075 g/cm and 0.010 g/cm. If the linear density of magnesium is

Teacher's Notes

greater than 0.010 g/cm, the volume of hydrogen generated in this reaction will exceed the 10-mL capacity of the graduated cylinder. Check to make sure that the 1-cm length of magnesium ribbon recommended in this experiment will not generate more than 10 mL of hydrogen gas. If necessary, cut back on the length of magnesium. For best results, use fresh magnesium ribbon or buff it with steel wool before weighing it.

- The concentration and volume of hydrochloric acid should be controlled variables. Optimum results were obtained using 5 mL of 2 M HCl, as recommended in the procedure. Using a smaller volume of more concentrated 3 M acid gave a more rapid reaction but the results were less reproducible.

- Not all graduated cylinders are created equal. We found that the best results were obtained using glass, tall-form, 10-mL graduated cylinders marked with 0.1-mL minor increments. Economy-choice graduated cylinders are shorter and are marked only in 0.2-mL minor increments—these are not recommended.

- If a barometer is not available in the lab or classroom, students may consult an Internet site such as the national weather service site (http://weather.gov/) to obtain a current "sea-level" pressure reading for your area. Note that these are NOT actual barometric pressure readings. Meteorologists convert station pressure values to what they would be if they had been taken at sea level. The following equation can be used to recalculate the barometric pressure (in inches Hg) from the reported sea-level pressure (in inches Hg). Elevation must be in meters.

$$\text{barometric pressure} = \text{sea-level pressure} - (\text{elevation}/312)$$

- The hydrogen gas may be collected in an ice-water bath at 0–5 °C rather than a room temperature water bath. This will reduce the size of the water-vapor contribution to the pressure and will also decrease the magnitude of the temperature correction in converting the measured volume to STP. If you live at high altitudes, or if the weather is stormy due to a low-pressure air mass, the experiment should definitely be carried out at 0–5 °C! Otherwise, the volume of hydrogen will exceed the 10-mL capacity of the graduated cylinder.

Teaching Tips

- For an alternative lab activity dealing with molar volume and applications of the ideal gas law, see the demonstration "Molar Mass of Butane." This demonstration uses disposable butane lighters to generate a measured mass of butane gas. The molar mass is calculated based on its theoretical molar volume.

- See "Construction of Gas Volume Cubes" in the *Demonstrations* section of this lab manual for a follow-up assessment activity. Different groups of students are assigned different numbers of moles of gas and are asked to construct a cube to represent the volume of the given number of moles of gas at STP. The examples have been chosen so that all of the cubes will have dimensions to the nearest centimeter (e.g., 0.0446 moles of gas will have a volume of 1.00 L at STP, corresponding to a cube 10.0 cm in length on each side).

Teacher's Notes

Teacher Notes

- Ask your students to come up with a list of interesting questions regarding the amount of gas in familiar, everyday objects. The questions (and answers) can be assigned as extra credit to reinforce gas law calculations or to prepare for tests. How much helium gas is needed to fill the Goodyear blimp? How much gas is present in an aerosol container pressurized at 2.2 atm? How many air molecules does it take to blow up a party balloon? What volume of butane gas would be generated if all the liquid butane in a barbecue lighter were converted to gas at STP?

Answers to Pre-Lab Questions *(Student answers will vary.)*

Reaction of 0.028 g of magnesium with excess hydrochloric acid generated 31.0 mL of hydrogen gas. The gas was collected by water displacement in a water bath 22 °C. The barometric pressure in the lab that day was 746 mm Hg.

1. Use Dalton's law and the vapor pressure of water at 22 °C (Table 1) to calculate the partial pressure of hydrogen gas in the gas collecting tube.

   Vapor pressure of water at 22 °C = 19.8 mm Hg

   $P_{total} = 746\ mm = P_{H_2} + 19.8\ mm\ Hg$

   $P_{H_2} = 746 - 19.8\ mm = 726\ mm\ Hg$

2. Use the combined gas law to calculate the "corrected" volume of hydrogen at STP. *Hint:* Watch your units for temperature and pressure!

   STP = 273 K (0 °C) and 1 atm

   $P_1 = 726\ mm\ Hg \times \dfrac{1\ atm}{760\ mm\ Hg} = 0.955\ atm \qquad P_2 = 1\ atm$

   $V_1 = 31.0\ mL\ (0.0310\ L) \qquad\qquad V_2 =$ "corrected" volume unknown

   $T_1 = 22\ °C + 273 = 295\ K \qquad\qquad T_2 = 273\ K$

   $\dfrac{P_1 V_1}{T_1} = \dfrac{P_2 V_2}{T_2}$

   Rearrange to solve for the unknown, $V_2 = \dfrac{P_1 V_1 T_2}{P_2 T_1}$

   $V_2 = \dfrac{(0.955\ atm)(0.0310\ L)(273\ K)}{(1\ atm)(295\ K)} = 0.0274\ L$

3. What is the theoretical number of moles of hydrogen that can be produced from 0.028 g of Mg? *Hint:* Refer to Equation 1 for the balanced equation for the reaction.

   Theoretical number of moles hydrogen = number of moles of magnesium used

   Number of moles of Mg $= 0.028\ g \times \dfrac{1\ mole}{24.3\ g} = 0.0012\ moles$

4. Divide the corrected volume of hydrogen by the theoretical number of moles of hydrogen to calculate the molar volume (in L/mole) of hydrogen at STP.

   Molar volume = 0.0274 L/0.0012 moles = 23 L/mole

Teacher's Notes

Sample Data

Student data will vary.

Data Table

	Trial 1	Trial 2	Trial 3*
Length of Mg Ribbon	1.0 cm	1.0 cm	1.0 cm
Mass of Mg	0.0094 g	0.0094 g	0.0094 g
Evidence of Chemical Reaction	The Mg metal disappeared and bubbles of gas were observed when the metal came in contact with the acid. The water drained out of the inverted graduated cylinder as the gas bubbles filled the tube.		
Volume of H$_2$ Gas	9.50 mL	9.90 mL	9.40 mL
Corrected Volume of H$_2$	9.30 mL	9.70 mL	9.20 mL
Temperature of Water Bath	23 °C	22 °C	22 °C
Barometric Pressure	764 mm Hg	764 mm Hg	764 mm Hg

*The results of three trials are shown here to illustrate the reproducibility of the method. Only two trials are required in the *Procedure*.

Answers to Post-Lab Calculations and Analysis *(Student answers will vary.)*

See the Sample Results Table on page 41 for the results of the calculations.

1. Calculate the theoretical number of moles of hydrogen gas produced in Trials 1 and 2.

    Theoretical number of moles of H$_2$ = number of moles of Mg

    For Trials 1 and 2: Number of moles of Mg $= \dfrac{0.0094 \text{ g}}{24.3 \text{ g/mole}} = 3.9 \times 10^{-4}$ *moles*

2. Use Table 1 in the Background section to find the vapor pressure of water at the temperature of the water bath in this experiment. Calculate the partial pressure of hydrogen gas produced in Trials 1 and 2.

    For Trial 1: Vapor pressure of water at 23 °C = 21.0 mm

    $P_{total} = 764 \text{ mm Hg} = P_{H_2} + 21 \text{ mm Hg}$

    $P_{H_2} = 764 \text{ mm Hg} - 21 \text{ mm Hg} = 743 \text{ mm Hg}$ (0.978 atm)

Teacher's Notes

3. Use the combined gas law to convert the measured volume of hydrogen to the volume the gas would occupy at STP for Trials 1 and 2. *Hint:* Remember the units!

$$V_2 = \frac{P_1 V_1 T_2}{P_2 T_1}$$

For Trial 1: $V_2 = \dfrac{(0.978 \text{ atm})(0.00930 \text{ L})(273 K)}{(1 \text{ atm})(296 \text{ K})} = 0.00839 \text{ L}$

4. Divide the volume of hydrogen gas at STP by the theoretical number of moles of hydrogen to calculate the molar volume of hydrogen for Trials 1 and 2.

For Trial 1: Molar volume = 0.00839 L/0.00039 moles = 22 L/mole

Sample Results Table

Number of moles of H_2 gas	3.9×10^{-4} moles	3.9×10^{-4} moles	3.9×10^{-4} moles
Vapor pressure of water	21.0 mm	19.8 mm	19.8 mm
Partial pressure of H_2 gas	743 mm	744 mm	744 mm
Calculated volume of H_2 gas at STP	0.00839 L	0.00865 L	0.00833 L
Molar volume of H_2 gas	22 L/mole	23 L/mole	22 L/mole
Average molar volume		22 L/mole	

5. What is the average value of the molar volume of hydrogen? Look up the literature value of the molar volume of a gas in your textbook and calculate the percent error in your experimental determination of the molar volume of hydrogen.

$$\text{Percent error} = \frac{|\text{Experimental value} - \text{Literature value}|}{\text{Literature value}} \times 100\%$$

Average molar volume = 22 L/mole (two significant figures)

Literature value of molar volume = 22.4 L/mole

$$\text{Percent error} = \frac{|22 \text{ L/mole} - 22.4 \text{ L/mole}|}{22.4 \text{ L/mole}} \times 100\% = 2\%$$

6. One mole of hydrogen gas has a mass of 2.02 g. Use your value of the molar volume of hydrogen to calculate the mass of one liter of hydrogen gas at STP. This is the density of hydrogen in g/L. How does this experimental value of the density compare with the literature value? (Consult a chemistry handbook for the density of hydrogen.)

$$\text{Calculated density} = \frac{1 \text{ mole} \times 2.02 \text{ g/mole}}{22 \text{ L}} = 0.092 \text{ g/L}$$

The literature value for the density of hydrogen gas is 0.0899 g/L at STP.

Teacher's Notes

7. In setting up this experiment, a student noticed that a bubble of air leaked into the graduated cylinder when it was inverted in the water bath. What effect would this have on the measured volume of hydrogen gas? Would the calculated molar volume of hydrogen be too high or too low as a result of this error? Explain.

   The bubble of air that leaked in would cause the measured volume of hydrogen to be too high. Both the calculated volume of hydrogen at STP and the molar volume would be too high as a result of this error.

8. A student noticed that the magnesium ribbon appeared to be oxidized—the metal surface was black and dull rather than silver and shiny. What effect would this error have on the measured volume of hydrogen gas? Would the calculated molar volume of hydrogen be too high or too low as a result of this error? Explain.

   Oxidation of magnesium converts the metal to magnesium oxide (MgO). The magnesium oxide coating would still react with hydrochloric acid, but would not generate hydrogen gas. The combined reaction of Mg and MgO with HCl would generate less hydrogen than the reaction of Mg alone. Both the calculated volume of hydrogen at STP and the molar volume would be too low as a result of this error. **Note to teachers:** *The black coating may be due to Mg_3N_2 or MgS.*

9. *(Optional)* Your teacher wants to scale up this experiment for demonstration purposes and would like to collect the gas in an inverted 50-mL buret. Use the ideal gas law to calculate the maximum length of magnesium ribbon that your teacher should use.

   Assume that the maximum volume of hydrogen gas which we can measure is 50 mL at a maximum "room" temperature of 30 °C (303 K) and a minimum atmospheric pressure of 0.95 atm. Substitute these values into the ideal gas equation to solve for n, the maximum number of moles of magnesium that can be used in the experiment.

   $n = PV/RT$

   $$n = \frac{(0.95 \text{ atm})(0.050 \text{ L})}{(0.0821 \text{ L atm/mole K})(303 \text{ K})} = 0.0019 \text{ moles Mg}$$

   Mass of magnesium = 0.0019 moles × 24.3 g/mole = 0.046 g

   Length of magnesium = 0.046 g/0.094 g/cm = 4.9 cm

   Note to teachers: *Assuming a higher than average temperature and a lower than normal atmospheric pressure gives us a maximum volume of hydrogen gas. This leaves some "wiggle room" for experimental error so that the actual volume will not exceed the capacity of the 50-mL buret.*

Teacher Notes

Technology and the Forgotten Gas Law
Pressure versus Temperature

Introduction

Avogadro, Boyle, Charles—these scientists and their gas laws are well known. Together their work defined the relationships among the four measurable gas properties, pressure, volume, temperature, and the number of moles of gas. Among the contributions of these scientists, the experiments by Amontons describing the effect of temperature on the pressure of a gas have largely been forgotten. Let's see how modern technology can help us rediscover the forgotten gas law and the relationship between pressure and temperature.

Concepts

- Boyle's law
- Absolute zero
- Amontons's law
- Kinetic–molecular theory

Background

The systematic study of gases began almost 350 years ago with Robert Boyle and his experiments on the relationship between the pressure and volume of air. Based on measurements of how the pressure of air changed as it was compressed and expanded, Boyle derived the mathematical relationship that today bears his name. According to Boyle's law, the pressure of a gas is inversely proportional to its volume if the temperature is held constant. In studying the behavior of gases, Robert Boyle was also aware of the effect of heat on gases, namely, that gases tended to expand when heated. Since no temperature scale existed at the time, Boyle lacked a mathematical means of relating the "hotness" of a gas to its volume or pressure.

In 1702, the French physicist Guillaume Amontons invented the air thermometer to measure temperature changes based on an increase in the volume of a gas as it was heated. This is essentially the principle behind Charles's law. Amontons also measured the pressure of a fixed volume of air as it was heated from room temperature to the temperature of boiling water. The relationship between the temperature and pressure of a gas is known as Amontons's law—the pressure of a gas is proportional to its temperature if the volume and the amount of the gas are held constant.

Experiment Overview

The purpose of this technology-based experiment is to carry out a modern version of Amontons's original experiments relating the pressure and temperature of a gas. The experiment will be carried out by trapping a fixed volume of air inside a flask at about 80 °C. The flask will be sealed, equipped with a pressure sensor, and gradually cooled in a series of steps in a water bath. The temperature of the bath will be measured using a temperature sensor. As the temperature decreases, the pressure of the air sample trapped inside the flask will also change. The mathematical relationship between temperature and pressure will be derived by plotting the data on a graph.

Technology and the Forgotten Gas Law – Page 2

Pre-Lab Questions

1. One of the reasons Amontons's law is often ignored is that it can be derived by combining Boyle's law and Charles's law. Combine the equations for Boyle's law ($P \times V$ = constant) and Charles's law (V/T = constant) to obtain the mathematical relationship for Amontons's law. *Note:* The Charles's law equation is only valid if the temperature is expressed in kelvins on the absolute temperature scale.

2. The gas laws explain how gases behave, but do not explain why. According to the kinetic-molecular theory (KMT), the temperature of a gas is a measure of the average kinetic energy of the gas particles—how fast they are moving. Collisions of the fast-moving gas particles with the container give rise to the pressure, defined as the force of these collisions divided by the area. Use the KMT to predict how the pressure of a gas will change when the gas is heated in a fixed-volume container.

3. The "Egg in the Bottle" is a favorite demonstration of many chemistry teachers. In this demonstration, a piece of burning paper is placed inside a bottle and a peeled, hard-boiled egg is placed over the bottle's mouth as soon as the fire burns out. As the bottle cools, the egg is forced into the bottle. Use Amontons's law to explain how this demonstration works.

Materials

Beakers, 400-mL and 1-L, 1 each	Pressure sensor and attached tubing*
Beral-type pipet, jumbo	Pressure relief valve (stopcock)*
Clamp, 1	Rubber stopper, two-hole, with adapters*
Computer interface system (LabPro)	Support (ring) stand
Computer or calculator for data analysis	Temperature sensor
Data collection software (LoggerPro)	Water
Erlenmeyer flask, Pyrex®, 125-mL	Thermometer (optional)
Hot plate	Tray (optional)
Ice	Gloves, heat-resistant

*The pressure sensor is attached via a plastic connector to a short length of tubing that has a second plastic connector at the other end. The sensor also comes equipped with a relief valve and stopper. See Figure 1.

Safety Precautions

The Erlenmeyer flask will develop a slight vacuum as the hot air inside the flask cools. Use only Pyrex® flasks with heavy-duty rims and carefully check the flask before use for chips or cracks. Make sure that the flask is securely held in the water bath and that it is not touching the sides or bottom of the beaker. Work carefully to avoid hitting or bumping the flask. Wear heat-resistant gloves and use caution when working with the hot water bath to avoid scalding or burns. Wear chemical splash goggles at all times when working with chemicals, glassware or heat in the laboratory.

Call or write us at Flinn Scientific to obtain a complimentary copy of the "Egg in the Bottle" demonstration.

Teacher Notes

Procedure

Preparation

1. Fill a 1-L beaker about ¾-full with water and heat the water on a hot plate at a medium-high setting to obtain a water-bath temperature of about 80 °C. *Note:* Turn down the setting on the hot plate as needed to avoid overheating the water.

2. If necessary, assemble the pressure sensor as follows. Attach the pressure sensor to a connector at one end of a piece of plastic tubing. Attach the connector at the other end of the tubing to one of the adapters in the two-hole rubber stopper. Attach the pressure relief valve to the second adapter in the two-hole rubber stopper.

3. Open the data collection software and connect the interface system to the computer or calculator. Plug the temperature sensor (Channel 1) and the pressure sensor (Channel 2) into the interface.

4. Set up the interface system for remote data collection.
   - Select *Setup* and *Data Collection* from the main screen, then choose *Selected Events* from the *Mode* menu.
   - Select *Set Up LabPro* from the *Remote* menu. Follow the on-screen instructions.
   - Save the experiment file so that it can be used later to retrieve the data from the interface.
   - Disconnect the interface from the computer.

Part A. Collecting the Data

5. Place the interface system with its attached sensors and rubber-stopper assembly on the lab bench where the hot water bath has been prepared.

6. Open the pressure relief valve on the rubber stopper assembly and place the stopper securely into a dry, 125-mL Erlenmeyer flask.

7. Immerse the flask in the hot water bath at 80 °C and clamp the rubber-stopper assembly to a ring stand. The flask should be submerged to the height of the rubber stopper. Do not allow the flask to touch the bottom or sides of the beaker (see Figure 1). *Note:* Make sure the pressure relief valve (stopcock) on the rubber stopper assembly is open during this time.

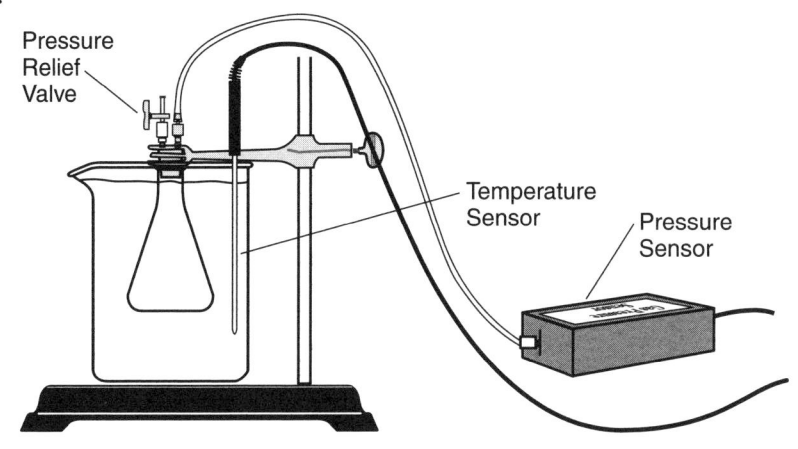

Figure 1.

The instructions in step 4 will vary depending on the interface system that is being used. The experiment as written was carried out using a Vernier LabPro™ interface with LoggerPro™ software.

Technology and the Forgotten Gas Law – Page 4

8. With the pressure relief valve open, allow the air inside the flask to adjust to the temperature of the water bath. Place the temperature sensor in the water bath and clamp it if needed.

9. After 3–5 minutes, close the pressure relief valve and press the *Start/Stop* button on the interface. A light on the interface should blink as the interface takes the first temperature and pressure reading.

10. Turn off the hot plate and unplug it. Wearing heat-resistant gloves, carefully remove the hot water bath from the hot plate and place it on a tray (optional) to collect any spillover water. Lower the flask and temperature sensor back into the hot water bath.

11. Add a few ice cubes to the hot water to lower the bath temperature. Monitor the temperature of the water bath with a thermometer. Remove excess water as needed using the jumbo, Beral-type pipet.

12. When the temperature of the bath is about 65 °C, press the *Start/Stop* button on the interface to take a second pressure–temperature reading.

13. Continue adding ice (and removing excess water as needed) to lower the temperature more quickly. Take a series of pressure and temperature readings (at least five) between 65 °C and 5 °C. Wait about a minute at each desired temperature before pressing the *Start/Stop* button.

14. When all of the data has been collected, open the pressure relief valve on the flask and unplug the sensors from the interface.

15. Remove the rubber stopper assembly from the flask and dismantle the apparatus as needed.

Part B. Analyzing the Data

16. Open the saved experiment file on the computer and reconnect the interface system to the computer.

17. Select *Retrieve Data* from the *Remote* menu. The data will automatically be graphed and displayed in a table. Click on the x-axis in the graph to select temperature as the x-axis (independent) variable. Click on the y-axis to select pressure as the y-axis (dependent) variable.

18. Click on the lowest and highest values on each axis to rescale the graph. Set the x-axis scale from –300 °C to 100 °C, the y-axis scale from 0 kPa to 120 kPa.

19. Select *Linear Fit-Best Curve Fit* from the *Analyze* menu to draw the best-fit straight line through the data.

Teacher Notes

Ideally, the water bath should be stirred to ensure even cooling. However, this is not practical with this setup. The Sample Data was collected without stirring—this may be considered a source of error.

Teacher Notes

Name: _____

Class/Lab Period: _____

Technology and the Forgotten Gas Law

Data Table*

Temperature (°C)	Pressure (kPa)	Temperature (K)†

*Computer-generated data tables and graphs may be substituted for the data table and Post-Lab Questions #1 and 5.

†See Post-Lab Question #5.

Post-Lab Questions

1. Plot or obtain a graph of pressure on the y-axis versus temperature on the x-axis. *Note:* See the *Procedure* section for the recommended scale for each axis.

2. Looking at the data, is the pressure of a gas proportional to its temperature over the temperature range studied? Use a computer or calculator to generate the best-fit straight line through the data points.

3. Extend the straight line backwards to estimate the x-intercept, the point at which the line crosses the x-axis. The x-intercept corresponds to absolute zero—the minimum temperature that would be needed to reduce the pressure of a gas to zero. What is the estimated value of absolute zero? How close is your value of absolute zero to the accepted value?

Technology and the Forgotten Gas Law – Page 6

4. Another way to see how well the data fits Amontons's law is to plot pressure versus temperature in kelvins on the absolute temperature scale.

   (a) Convert each temperature reading to kelvins using the equation

   $T(K) = t(°C) + 273$.

   (b) Plot or obtain a graph of pressure in kPa on the y-axis versus temperature in kelvins on the x-axis.

   (c) Starting at the origin, draw a best-fit straight line through the data. The point (0,0) satisfies the condition that at absolute zero the pressure of the gas should be zero. How well does this line fit the data?

5. Amontons's law is explained on the basis of the kinetic-molecular theory for ideal gases. Would you expect to see greater deviations from ideal gas behavior at high or low temperatures? At high or low pressures? Explain.

6. The safety warnings on aerosol cans illustrate a real-world application of Amontons's law. Most aerosol cans will have a warning similar to the following:

   "Do not place in hot water or near radiators, stoves or other sources of heat. Do not puncture or incinerate container or store at temperatures over 120 °F."

   Use the results of this experiment to predict what will happen to the gas in an aerosol container at elevated temperatures and to explain why the warning label is needed.

Teacher's Notes
Technology and the Forgotten Gas Law

Master Materials List *(for a class of 30 students working in pairs)*

Beakers, 400-mL and 1-L, 15 each	Pressure sensors and attached tubing, 15*
Beral-type pipets, jumbo, 15	Pressure relief valves (stopcock), 15*
Clamps, 15	Rubber stoppers, two-hole, with adapters, 15*
Computer interface system (LabPro), 15	Support (ring) stands, 15
Computers or calculators for data analysis	Temperature sensors, 15
Data collection software (LoggerPro)	Water
Erlenmeyer flasks, Pyrex®, 125-mL, 15	Thermometers (optional), 15
Hot plates, 7	Trays (optional), 15
Ice	Gloves, heat-resistant, 5–7

*The pressure sensors and rubber stopper assemblies may be set up before class to save time. Do not dismantle them between classes.

Safety Precautions

The Erlenmeyer flask will develop a slight vacuum as the hot air inside the flask cools. Use only Pyrex® flasks with heavy-duty rims and carefully check the flask before use for chips or cracks. Make sure that the flask is securely held in the water bath and that it is not touching the sides or bottom of the beaker. Work carefully to avoid hitting or bumping the flask. Wear heat-resistant gloves and use caution when working with the hot water bath to avoid scalding or burns. Wear chemical splash goggles at all times when working with chemicals, glassware, or heat in the laboratory. Please consult the manufacturer's instructions for additional safety guidelines regarding the use of specific pressure and temperature sensors.

Disposal

All of the materials used in this laboratory are reusable—no disposal required.

Lab Hints

- The laboratory work for this experiment can reasonably be completed within an average 50-minute class period. To ensure an unhurried, safe lab environment, it may be helpful to use a second class period for data analysis. Have students download their data to the computer and save the file to work on later.

- A slight vacuum (80 kPa, about 600 mm Hg) will develop in the Erlenmeyer flask as the hot air is cooled. We recommend that you use only borosilicate (e.g., Pyrex®) flasks with heavy-duty rims. Do not use economy-choice flasks. Check the flasks for chips or cracks before setting them out for student use, and replace any that have imperfections.

Teacher's Notes

- As an alternative, this experiment has also been traditionally carried out by trapping the air first at room temperature and atmospheric pressure and then placing the flask in successively hotter or colder water baths. Starting with a sample of air at 20 °C and 100 kPa, we found that the pressure increased to 138 kPa at 91 °C and decreased to 94 kPa at 4 °C. After testing both experiment modifications, we recommend the procedure given in the student section. It involves less overall handling of the flask and the percent pressure difference between the inside and outside of the flask is also lower. In addition to improved safety, the recommended procedure offers greater accuracy.

- The rubber stopper assembly tends to pop out easily when the trapped air is heated above 85–90 °C. For this reason, we recommend starting the experiment at a maximum temperature of about 80 °C. Remind students that the recommended temperatures for data collection are approximate targets, not exact goals. Excellent results are obtained with as few as five data points spread out over the recommended temperature range.

- The units for the pressure sensor measurements can be selected by the user—the choices are kPa, mmHg, and atm. Kilopascals (kPa) are the SI units for pressure and are becoming standard in more high school chemistry tests. This lab provides a good opportunity to review all of the common units for pressure and where they are used.

- For a simpler technology-based lab, consider performing a Boyle's law experiment with a plastic syringe attached to the pressure sensor. The *Supplementary Information* section (pp. 55–56) gives instructions and sample data for a Boyle's law determination using the technology described in this experiment. This versatile experiment allows you to easily test different gases and different amounts of gases. Testing different gases reveals whether "real" gases follow ideal gas behavior.

Teaching Tips

- Amontons's law is probably the most often ignored gas law, and for that reason this lab is an excellent place to start the inquiry into the gas laws—students are more motivated if they feel they are doing something they have not seen or done before. As a technology-based experiment, this lab is also very valuable in that it allows students to do something they could not easily do without the technology. The use of the pressure sensor fills a real need and is tailor-made for gas law experiments.

- The relationship between pressure and temperature is sometimes referred to as Gay-Lussac's law instead. In some countries, however, Charles's law is also known as Gay-Lussac's law, so things can get more than a little confusing. What seems certain is that (1) Amontons developed the air thermometer design, and (2) he showed how the pressure of air changed as it was heated or cooled. Gay-Lussac is given credit for systematic measurements of both pressure and volume versus temperature and for the mathematical treatment of the gas laws.

- The study of the gas laws is a natural place to demonstrate that the *history* of science illuminates the *nature* of science, a formal goal in the National Science Education Standards. Our understanding of the behavior of gases did not arise in one "fell swoop" but rather as a result of small, incremental advances over a long period of time. More importantly, each small advance in knowledge would not have been possible without the previous work. In some cases, progress was made possible by an advance in a way of

Teacher's Notes

measuring something (pressure or temperature, etc.). In other cases, progress was made possible by an advance in a way of thinking about something (heat or temperature).

Answers to Pre-Lab Questions *(Student answers will vary.)*

1. One of the reasons Amontons's law is often ignored is that it can be derived by combining Boyle's law and Charles's law. Combine the equations for Boyle's law (P × V = constant) and Charles's law (V/T = constant) to obtain the mathematical relationship for Amontons's law. *Note:* The Charles's law equation is only valid if the temperature is expressed in kelvins on the absolute temperature scale.

   For a fixed amount of gas, Boyle's law and Charles's law refer to different conditions (constant T vs. constant P, respectively).

   $$V = \frac{k_1}{P} \quad \text{(at constant T)}$$

   $$V = k_2 \times T \quad \text{(at constant P)}$$

   These relationships may be combined as follows:

   $$V = k_3 \times \frac{T}{P}$$

   For a fixed amount of gas at constant V, Amontons's law may be written as

   T/P = constant or P/T = constant

2. The gas laws explain how gases behave, but do not explain why. According to the kinetic-molecular theory (KMT), the temperature of a gas is a measure of the average kinetic energy of the gas particles—how fast they are moving. Collisions of the fast-moving gas particles with the container give rise to the pressure, defined as the force of these collisions divided by the area. Use the KMT to predict how the pressure of a gas will change when the gas is heated in a fixed-volume container.

   The average kinetic energy of the gas particles increases as the temperature increases. Since the mass of the particles does not change, their velocity must increase. As the particles move faster in the same-size container, the force per collision will increase. Since the pressure is due to the force exerted per unit area, the pressure of the gas will increase as the gas is heated.

3. The "Egg in the Bottle" is a favorite demonstration of many chemistry teachers. In this demonstration, a piece of burning paper is placed inside a bottle and a peeled, hard-boiled egg is placed over the bottle's mouth as soon as the fire burns out. As the bottle cools, the egg is forced into the bottle. Use Amontons's law to explain how this demonstration works.

   Burning the paper heats the air inside the open bottle and causes the gas to expand and some of it to escape from the bottle. When the fire burns out, the remaining air is trapped in the bottle by the egg and subsequently cools down. As the temperature of the air in the bottle decreases, so does the gas pressure inside the bottle relative to that of the surrounding air outside the bottle. The greater pressure (force) of the outside air forces the egg into the flask. It is both the lower temperature and the fewer number of moles of air that cause the egg to be pushed into the bottle.

Teacher's Notes

Sample Data

Teacher Notes

Student data will vary.

Data Table

Temperature (°C)	Pressure (kPa)	Temperature (K)†
82.5	102.3	355.7
74.7	100.0	347.9
54.1	94.8	327.3
47.1	92.8	320.3
34.5	89.4	307.7
22.3	86.3	295.5
11.6	83.5	284.8
3.0	80.4	276.2

†See *Post-Lab* Question #4.

Answers to Post-Lab Questions *(Student answers will vary.)*

1. Plot or obtain a graph of pressure on the y-axis versus temperature on the x-axis. *Note:* See the *Procedure* section for the recommended scale for each axis.

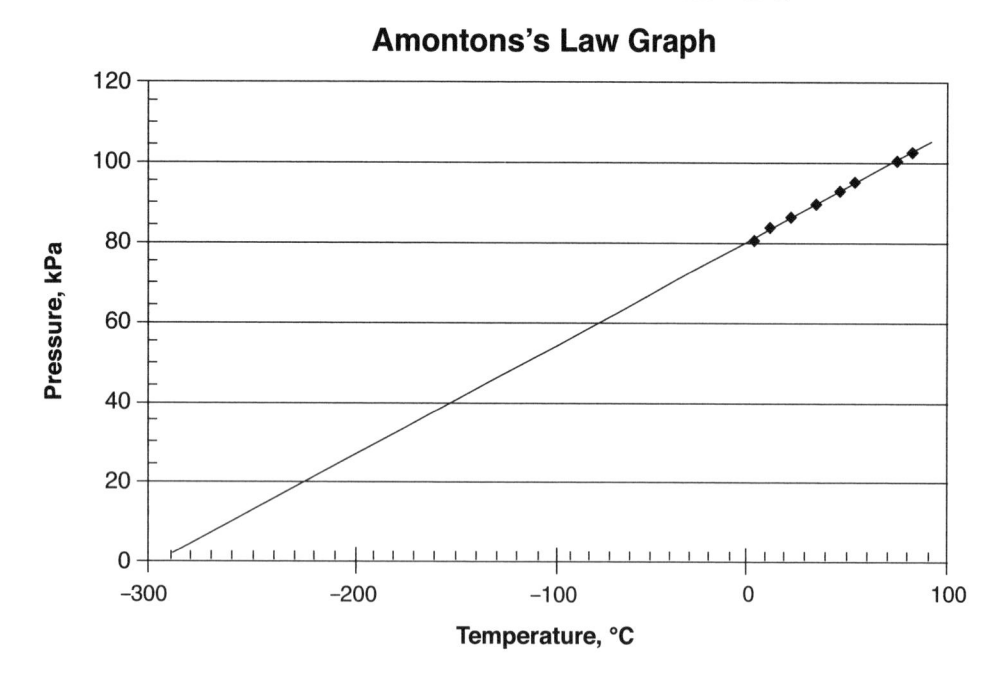

Amontons's Law Graph

Flinn ChemTopic™ Labs — The Gas Laws

Teacher's Notes

Teacher Notes

2. Looking at the data, is the pressure of a gas proportional to its temperature over the temperature range studied? Use a computer or calculator to generate the best-fit straight line through the data points.

   A plot of temperature versus pressure gives an excellent straight line through the data points. This means that the pressure of the gas is proportional to temperature over the entire temperature range studied. See the graph for the best-fit straight line.

3. Extend the straight line backwards to estimate the x-intercept, the point at which the line crosses the x-axis. The x-intercept corresponds to absolute zero—the minimum temperature that would be needed to reduce the pressure of a gas to zero. What is the estimated value of absolute zero? How close is your value of absolute zero to the accepted value?

   The estimated value of absolute zero is –290 °C.

4. Another way to see how well the data fits Amontons's law is to plot pressure versus temperature in kelvins on the absolute temperature scale.

   (a) Convert each temperature reading to kelvins using the equation

   $T(K) = t(°C) + 273.$

   See the Sample Data Table.

   (b) Plot or obtain a graph of pressure in kPa on the y-axis versus temperature in kelvins on the x-axis.

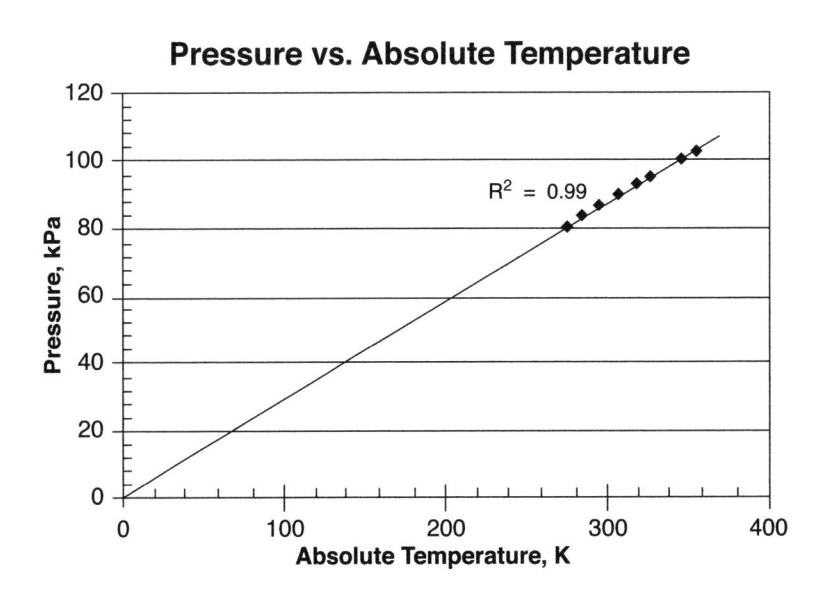

Pressure vs. Absolute Temperature

$R^2 = 0.99$

Technology and the Forgotten Gas Law

Teacher's Notes

(c) Starting at the origin, draw a best-fit straight line through the data. The point (0,0) satisfies the condition that at absolute zero the pressure of the gas should be zero. How well does this line fit the data?

The fit is excellent! **Note to teachers:** *The correlation coefficient of 0.99 shows the accuracy of this method. The contrast with the value of absolute zero predicted in the first graph also shows that very, very small differences in the straight line through the data points leads to very large differences in the extrapolated value of absolute zero. This is because the data points are so far away from the point we are looking for.*

5. Amontons's law is explained on the basis of the kinetic-molecular theory for ideal gases. Would you expect to see greater deviations from ideal gas behavior at high or low temperatures? At high or low pressures? Explain.

    *Deviations from ideal gas behavior become more important at **low temperatures** and at **high pressures**. At low temperatures, attractive forces between the gas molecules become more important (remember, in the KMT the presence of attractive forces is ignored). At high temperatures, gas particles have large kinetic energies, which helps them "overcome" the attractive forces between molecules. At high pressures, the gas particles are forced closer together and the attractive forces between them become stronger.*

6. The safety warnings on aerosol cans illustrate a real-world application of Amontons's law. Most aerosol cans will have a warning similar to the following:

    "Do not place in hot water or near radiators, stoves or other sources of heat. Do not puncture or incinerate container or store at temperatures over 120 °F."

Use the results of this experiment to predict what will happen to the gas in an aerosol container at elevated temperatures and to explain why the warning label is needed.

An aerosol can is a constant volume container and is already "pressurized" (the internal pressure is about 2.5 atm). At high temperatures, the pressure of the gas inside the container will increase to an unacceptably high level and the container essentially becomes a bomb ready to explode. **Note to teachers:** *There is a second reason for the safety warning. Many aerosols contain flammable gas propellants which will ignite when released suddenly at high temperatures.*

Teacher's Notes

Teacher Notes

Supplementary Information

Boyle's Law Determination Using the Pressure Sensor

1. Connect the interface system to the computer or calculator and plug the pressure sensor into Channel 1 (CH 1) of the interface.

2. Draw 10.0 mL of air (or other gas) into a 20-mL syringe and attach the syringe to the pressure sensor.

3. Select *Setup and Sensors* from the main screen and choose "Pressure." Click on the desired units of pressure.

4. Open a new file from the File Menu to set up a live readout and data table for pressure–volume measurements. The window should include a graph of pressure on the y-axis versus volume on the x-axis.

5. Select *Setup* followed by *Data Collection*. Click on *Events with Entry* to set the computer for manual sampling. Enter "Volume" and the appropriate units in the Column Label box.

6. Press *Collect* on the main screen to begin pressure readings.

7. When the pressure reading stablizes, press *Keep* on the main screen to automatically record the pressure measurement. Type the gas volume (10.0 mL) in the Edit box, then press *Enter* to save this P–V data pair.

8. Move the syringe plunger to position the black rubber gasket seal at the 5.0-mL line.

9. When the pressure reading stabilizes, press *Keep* and type the gas volume (5.0 mL) in the Edit box. Press *Enter* to save the P–V data pair.

10. Repeat steps 8 and 9 to obtain pressure readings at gas volumes of 7.5, 12.5, 15.0, 17.5, and 20.0 mL.

11. Press *Stop* on the main screen to end the data collection process.

12. If possible, obtain a printout of the data table and graph.

13. Analyze the pressure–volume data to determine the mathematical relationship.

See page 56 for P–V sample graphs obtained using this method.

Technology and the Forgotten Gas Law

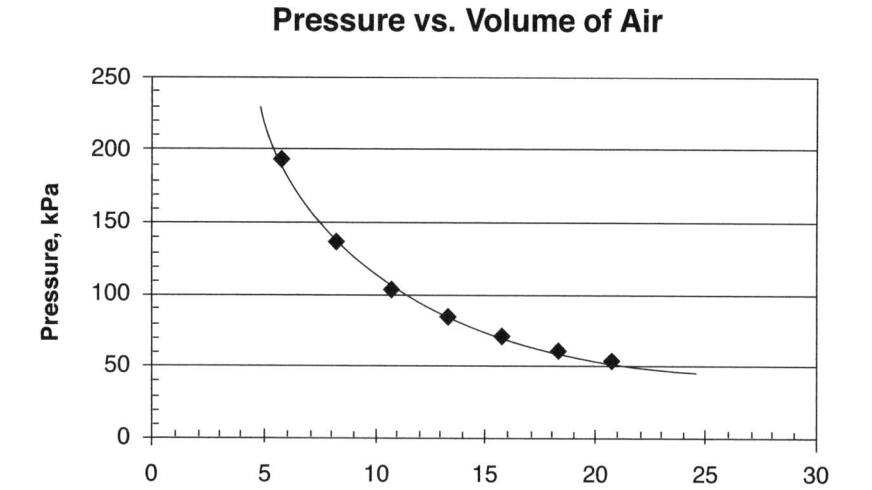

Teacher's Notes

Pressure vs. Volume of Air

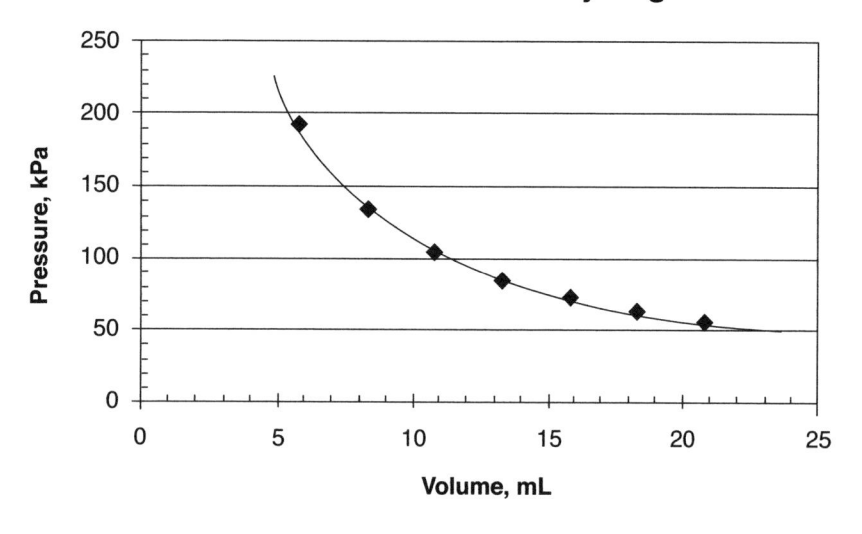

Pressure vs. Volume of Hydrogen

Teacher Notes

Life on Planet V
A Classroom Activity

Introduction

What would it be like to live in a vacuum? Which of our tools and toys would still work the same? Which would work better? Which would not work at all?

Concepts

- Atmospheric pressure
- Vacuum

Overview of the Activity

Discuss the fact that there is no such thing as suction—things do not get pulled or sucked by a vacuum, but instead they get pushed from the other side by atmospheric pressure. After performing a classic pressure vs. vacuum demonstration such as "The Collapsing Can," use this "mental lab" activity to stimulate further discussion and understanding of this concept. The debates that result are sure to lead to some of the best learning of the year!

Procedure

Imagine you have been relocated to Planet V, a planet just like Earth, but with no atmosphere at all. Which of the items listed below would still work on this planet and which items would not work? For those items that would work, would they work exactly the same? For those items that would not work, can you think of modifications that would enable them to work? Be prepared to defend your answers!

suction cup	parachute	drinking straw
candle	pogo stick	broom
match	swing	alarm clock
flashlight	automobile	shotgun
vacuum cleaner	air bag	radio
paper airplane	balloon	bow and arrow
helicopter	paint	star
rocket	blow dryer	bicycle pump
aerosol spray can	Frisbee	flag
baseball and bat	TNT	golf
nuclear fuel rod	light stick	squirt gun
plant	siphon	refrigerator
syringe	smoke detector	magnet

Use this page as a student handout, if desired.

Life on Planet V – Page 2

Discussion

There are no clear-cut, yes or no answers for many of the items. The purpose is not to get the right answer, but to get students thinking about the role that the atmospheric pressure plays in everyday life.

Suction cup: No, since there's no pressure to push it against the wall, it wouldn't stick.

Candle: No, since combustion requires oxygen.

Match: Yes, for a short while, since it supplies its own oxygen from the decomposition of potassium chlorate.

Flashlight: Yes, light does not require air.

Vacuum cleaner: No. The motor would run, but it would serve no purpose without atmospheric pressure to push the dirt in.

Paper airplane: It would not glide, turn or do flips, it would just follow a straight trajectory path, flipping end over end like a thrown stick.

Helicopter: No. The engine would not start without oxygen, and even if it were electric, it still could not lift off.

Rocket: Yes, obviously, since they are used in space, which is a vacuum. Like a match, rockets supply their own oxygen (the space shuttle, for example, uses hydrogen and oxygen). Also rockets do not need to push on air the way airplanes and helicopters do, instead they work by propulsion.

Aerosol spray can: Yes since it supplies its own pressure, but the spray would spread out in a cone shape and travel out indefinitely. It would not form a mist or cloud.

Baseball and bat: Yes, the ball would fly further without air resistance but curve balls would not be possible.

Nuclear fuel rod: Yes, unlike combustion, fission requires no air. The chain reaction should still work fine and give off heat just as well.

Plant: No. Obviously with no air there would be no carbon dioxide available for photosynthesis.

Syringe: Yes and No. If the fluid is already in the syringe, it would be possible to expel it, but it would not be possible to draw liquid up into the syringe by simply pulling back on the plunger. The liquid would also pour out of the syringe if it was tipped.

Parachute: No, because there is no air, there would be no air resistance.

Pogo stick: Yes, should work fine. Many students confuse zero pressure with zero gravity and predict the pogo stick rider would never come down; this is a good opportunity to differentiate the two.

Swing: Yes, but with the swinger's hair would only move back and forth slightly due to inertia instead of blowing back and forth due to air resistance.

Teacher Notes

Teacher Notes

Automobile: No, unless it was electric; then it should work fine—there was a moon buggy used during the Apollo missions. There would be no need for any kind of aerodynamic design either: all shapes would be equally effective!

Air bag: Yes. A quick gas-producing chemical reaction inflates them.

Balloon: Yes, provided it could be filled from some tank of compressed gas, and it would not take very much gas to "fill" the balloon either. The notion that any air inside the balloon would cause it to pop ignores the pressure exerted by the elasticity of the balloon material itself. Without air resistance, however, the balloon would fall as quickly as a stone!

Paint: Yes and no: some students argue that the paint would never dry without air, and it is easy to see where this comes from since blowing air on something makes it dry even faster. Yet drying relies on evaporation, and evaporation is actually hindered by air. In fact, drying would happen almost instantaneously in a vacuum, and so it would be very difficult once a can of paint was opened to have time to get it onto the surface! Spray paint might even dry to a powder before it reaches its target!

Blow dryer: No, not unless it had some sort of compressed air attachment.

Frisbee: Yes and no: it could be thrown, and it could be spun, but there would be no gliding or floating or hooking action. It would fly more like a discus (and even those ride the air a bit).

TNT: Yes, but there is some disagreement on whether it would be as effective.

Light stick: Yes, the chemical reaction contained inside does not rely on air.

Siphon: No. Just like a drinking straw, a siphon depends on atmospheric pressure to do the pushing.

Smoke detector: Yes and no. The Geiger tube would still function, and the alpha emitter would still work. (Like fission and fusion, radioactive decay does not depend on air), but with no air to support it, the smoke would not become suspended, but instead would sink quickly straight downward. If the smoke detector were on the floor so that the smoke landed on it and blocked the path of the alpha particles, then the smoke detector would detect smoke, but you wouldn't hear the alarm! Some students question the need for a smoke detector in a place with no oxygen available to support combustion.

Drinking straw: No, even if we ignore the fact that liquids would tend to boil away at the low pressure, a drinking straw relies on atmospheric pressure to push and not sucking to pull.

Broom: Yes, but perhaps not as well, many students question to what extent sweeping relies on air currents to help push the dust.

Alarm clock: Yes, visually, but since sound requires air, the alarm sound would not reach your ears!

Shotgun: Yes, gunpowder also carries its own oxidizing agent, KNO_3, and the buckshot would shoot a lot further.

Life on Planet V – Page 4

Radio: Yes and no. The radio waves would still reach the radio but no sound would come out.

Bow and arrow: Yes and no. The bow would still be able to accelerate the arrow, and the arrow would actually fly much farther, but with no air drag to hold the fletching back, the arrow would turn end over end and likely not hit the target head first.

Star: Yes, of course. Stars already work just fine in the vacuum where they exist. Like fission, fusion does not need oxygen. This is a good opportunity to point out that stars are not burning the way a candle does.

Bicycle pump: No, since a pump takes air on the outside and forces it into the tire, the pump would have nothing to pump. Aerosol pumps, however, which are currently available, should still work fine.

Flag: Not if you're expecting it to wave! What about the American flag on the moon, all the photos make it look like its being held straight out? It is, by a support rod across the top!

Golf: Yes, and you don't have to worry about the wind. Each drive would go farther and no more slicing or hooking the ball!

Squirt gun: Yes, I think, if the pump is pumping water out instead of air in.

Refrigerator: Yes and no. The entire cooling system is closed and works independently of any outside air, but with no air to carry the coldness from the cooling elements to the food nothing in the refrigerator would get refrigerated! The heating elements on the back of the refrigerator also rely on air to dissipate the heat.

Magnets: No problem here.

Demonstrations

Teacher Notes

The Collapsing Can
Pressure Is a Force Demonstration

Introduction

Pressure—we all feel it. But what is it? In the case of the surrounding air, the pressure it exerts is a force—a surprisingly strong force. Here's a pressure-packed demonstration that will convince students that air is a force to be reckoned with!

Concepts

- Atmospheric Pressure
- Kinetic-molecular theory
- Vacuum

Materials

Demonstration Version

Metal can with screw-top cap, 1-quart
Water
Hot plate
Zetex™ heat-resistant gloves or oven mitt

Student Version

Soda can, empty
Large dishpan or bowl
Water
Bunsen or alcohol burner
Beaker tongs

Safety Precautions

The hot can and escaping steam can cause severe burns. Wear protective gloves and use caution when handling the hot can. Never place your hands in the steam. Wear chemical splash goggles and heat-resistant gloves. Always practice a demonstration before presenting it to students.

Procedure

Demonstration Version

1. Obtain a metal can with an airtight, screwtop cap.

2. Remove the cap from the metal can. Be sure the can is clean and free of chemicals—a new, unused can is preferred. Rinse the can, if necessary, to remove any residual chemicals.

3. Add approximately 50 mL of tap water to the metal can. This should be enough to cover the bottom of the can to a depth of about 1 cm.

4. Place the can on a hot plate and heat it until the water boils and steam flows out of the uncapped opening.

5. Wear heat-resistant gloves, remove the steaming can from the hot plate. Place the can where it can be easily viewed.

6. Immediately place the cap on the can and close tightly.

7. Within a few minutes, the can suddenly will collapse in on itself as it is crushed by the force of the surrounding air. *Note:* The result may be a fairly loud implosion. Warn student to expect a sudden noise!

"The Collapsing Can" is available as a Chemical Demonstraton Kit from Flinn Scientific (Catalog No. AP4695).

Demonstrations

Student Version — Teacher Notes

1. Rinse out an empty 12-oz, aluminum soda can, then add about 15–20 mL of water into the can.

2. Fill a 1-L beaker, a large bowl, or a dishpan with 2–3 inches of water. Set the water near your burner.

3. Heat the can with a Bunsen or alcohol burner until the water comes to a boil and steam is coming out of the can. Hold the can with a pair of beaker tongs.

4. After steam has steadily come out of the can for 15–20 seconds, remove the can from the heat.

5. Immediately turn the can upside down and plunge the open end of the can into the container of water.

6. *Warning:* The can will immediately collapse with a loud noise and some water may splash out of the container.

Disposal

The crushed can may be disposed of in the normal trash.

Tips

- The cover on the can must be able to provide an airtight seal. Make sure the cap is screwed on tightly before allowing the can to cool.

- If a cap to the can is not available, try a rubber stopper. Be sure the rubber stopper fits snugly in the can opening.

- Place the collapsed can alongside an identical, un-crushed can in a classroom display case to provide a visual reminder of the invisible pressure of air.

Discussion

The tremendous force required to crush the can comes from the difference in pressure between the outside of the can (normal atmospheric pressure) and the partial vacuum created inside the can by the condensing steam. When the water inside the can boils, it is converted to steam, which drives the air out of the can. When the can is then capped and allowed to cool, the steam condenses back to a liquid. Since there are fewer air (gas) molecules remaining in the can than there were originally, the gas pressure inside the can—after it cools— is substantially lower than that of the outside air. The pressure on the outside of the can is normal atmospheric pressure (about 15 lb/in^2). The greater force on the outside of the can pushes in on the can and crushes it.

Flinn ChemTopic™ Labs — The Gas Laws

Demonstrations

Teacher Notes

Massing Gases
Avogadro's Law Demonstration

Introduction

Make Avogadro proud by using his law to determine the molar mass of several gases. Equal volumes of a reference gas and other gases will be trapped inside a syringe and their masses will be measured. By comparing their mass ratios, the molar mass of each gas can be determined.

Concepts

- Avogadro's law
- Molar mass
- Buoyancy

Materials

Luer-lock plastic syringe, 60-mL
Latex tubing and pinch clamp, 2
Medicine dropper, glass piece only, 2
Plastic freezer bags, quart size, 2
Nail

Rubber stopper, size 10, 2
Cork borer, 12–20 mm diameter
Balance, milligram (0.001 g precision),
Gas sources, several
Syringe tip cap

Safety Precautions

Wear chemical splash goggles, chemical-resistant gloves, and a chemical-resistant apron. Please consult current Material Safety Data Sheets for additional safety information.

Preparation

Construct the Gas Delivery Apparatus

1. Use a large, sharpened cork borer to cut a large hole (12–20 mm) in a size 10, one-hole rubber stopper. The result is a stopper with a plug that can be removed (the plug has the original single hole in it).

2. Remove the plug from the stopper and push the plastic bag through the hole in the stopper, leaving about 1 inch of the bag sticking out of the opening. (Figure 1.)

3. Place the smaller, one-hole stopper "plug" into the freezer bag opening. The freezer bag should now be held tightly between the walls of the two stoppers. (Figure 2.)

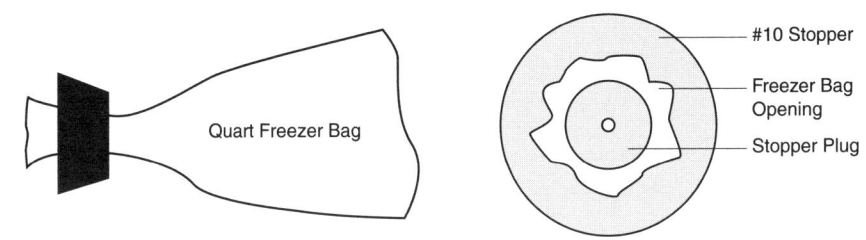

Figure 1. Side View   **Figure 2.** Top View

4. Carefully insert the tapered end of a medicine dropper through the small hole in the stopper plug. To do this, place a drop or two of glycerin in the hole and slowly work the dropper back and forth until the tip is inside the bag (Figure 3).

Massing Gases is available as a Chemical Demonstraton Kit from Flinn Scientific (Catalog No. AP6299).

Demonstrations

5. Attach a short piece of latex tubing over the top end of the medicine dropper and place the pinch clamp on the latex tubing. The apparatus is now complete.

Filling with a Gas

6. Evacuate the gas delivery apparatus: Remove the pinch clamp and attach the latex tubing to either a vacuum pump or an aspirator. When the bag has been evacuated, replace the pinch clamp on the tubing.

7. Attach the end of the latex tubing to the outlet of the gas source and remove the pinch clamp.

8. As slowly as possible, fill the gas delivery apparatus with the gas. The bag should be taut when filled, but not ready to burst.

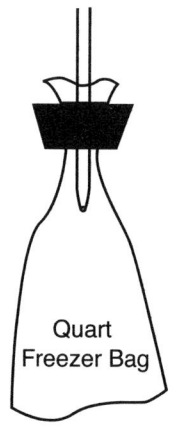

Figure 3. Assembly with Dropper

9. Turn off the gas source and replace the pinch clamp. The gas delivery apparatus now contains a slightly pressurized sample of gas.

10. Repeat steps 6–9 using a new gas delivery bag for each gas to be massed.

Preparing the Plastic Syringe

11. Pull the syringe out to the greatest volume that is marked on the barrel. For a 60-mL syringe this will be 60-mL.

12. Create a hole in the syringe plunger so that a nail will slide through the plunger and prevent it from being pulled into the syringe. Either heat the nail in a Bunsen burner and push it through the plunger or drill a hole using an electric drill (Figure 4).

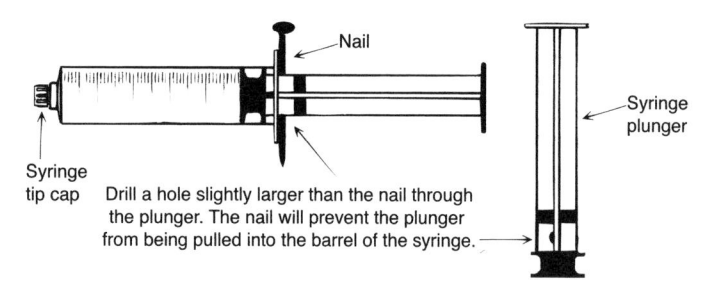

Figure 4.

Procedure

1. Completely push the plunger into the syringe. Attach the syringe tip cap to the tip of the syringe.

2. Pull the plunger to the preset mark and place the nail in the prepared hole in the plunger. The syringe plunger is now fully extended and the barrel of the syringe is under vacuum. *Note:* This step requires two people—one person pulls the plunger out past the preset mark and the other person inserts the nail into the prepared hole.

3. Measure and record the mass of the evacuated syringe assembly.

4. Remove the syringe tip cap to allow air to enter the syringe. Replace the syringe tip cap and find the mass of the syringe assembly filled with air. The plunger should still be "fully extended."

Assemble a new gas delivery apparatus for each gas to be measured.

Flinn ChemTopic™ Labs — The Gas Laws

Demonstrations

Teacher Notes

5. Remove the nail and the syringe tip cap. Depress the plunger to expel the air from the syringe.

6. Attach the syringe to the latex tubing of a gas delivery apparatus for the reference gas.

7. Release the pinch clamp and draw the reference gas into the syringe until the plunger is slightly past the preset mark.

8. Insert the nail into the hole in the plunger, then push the plunger forward so the nail rests on the syringe barrel.

9. Close off the gas delivery by closing the pinch clamp on the latex tubing.

10. Hold the plunger in while removing the latex tubing from the syringe. Immediately attach the syringe tip cap.

11. Measure and record the mass of the syringe assembly filled with the reference gas.

12. Remove the syringe tip cap and expel the gas. Repeat steps 5–12 with additional gas samples, as desired.

Sample Data

Mass of Evacuated Syringe Assembly ___76.931___ g

	Reference Gas (Oxygen)	Air	Nitrogen
Mass of Syringe Assembly and Gas	77.107 g	77.099 g	77.096 g
Mass of Gas	0.176 g	0.168 g	0.165 g
Mass of Gas/Mass of Reference Gas	1.00	0.955	0.938
Experimental Molar Mass		30.5 g/mole	30.0 g/mole
Accepted Molar Mass	32.0 g/mole	28.9 g/mole	28.0 g/mole
Percent Error		6%	7%

Disposal

Nitrogen, oxygen, air, etc. may be released into the atmosphere. Flammable or poisonous gases should be released inside an efficiently operating fume hood. Consult your current *Flinn Scientific Catalog/Reference Manual* for proper disposal procedures.

Tips

- There are various sources for gases to test. Propane and butane are available from hardware supply stores. Burner gas is a source of methane. Lecture bottles of many gases are available from Flinn Scientific.

- Step 2 in the *Procedure* section requires a large amount of force to pull the syringe plunger out. Keep fingers away from the plunger shaft to avoid pinching fingers if the plunger should slip.

- The higher the molar mass of the gas, the better the results. Propane and butane work well because they have higher molar masses.

If a milligram balance is not available, a centigram (0.01-g precision) balance may be used, although there will be some loss in accuracy. A centigram balance should not be used with the lightest gases, hydrogen and helium.

Massing Gases

Demonstrations

Discussion

Air, like water, exerts a positive or upward buoyant force on all objects. When massing gases, this force is substantial and the apparent mass of gas is less than the true mass of the gas. The difference in mass corresponds to the mass of air displaced by the gas.

$$\text{True mass of gas} = \text{apparent mass of gas} + \text{mass of air displaced}$$

By evacuating the syringe volume of all gas (steps 1–3), the last term, mass of air displaced, is eliminated and the true mass of the gas can be directly determined.

Avogadro's law states that the number of moles of a gas is directly proportional to its volume if the pressure and temperature are held constant.

$$n = kV \text{ (at constant } P, T) \qquad \textit{Equation 1}$$

$$k = P/RT$$

If equal volumes (V) of two gases (A and B) are measured at the same temperature and pressure, the two gases must have the same number of moles.

$$n_A = kV = n_B \text{ (at constant } P, T) \qquad \textit{Equation 2}$$

The number of moles of any gas is equal to the mass of the gas divided by its molar mass. Substituting this relationship into Equation 2 gives

$$\frac{\text{mass}_A}{\text{Molar mass}_A} = \frac{\text{mass}_B}{\text{Molar mass}_B}$$

or

$$\frac{\text{mass}_A}{\text{mass}_B} = \frac{\text{Molar mass}_A}{\text{Molar mass}_B} \qquad \textit{Equation 3}$$

If the molar mass of a reference gas is known, the molar mass of an "unknown" gas can be determined by comparing the masses of equal volumes of the two gases (Equation 3).

The Sample Data shows typical results obtained using oxygen as a reference gas. Air and nitrogen were used as unknowns. The experimental molar mass of air was calculated as follows:

$$\text{Molar mass}_{air} = \frac{0.168 \text{ g}}{0.176 \text{ g}} \times 32.0 \text{ g/mole} = 30.5 \text{ g/mole}$$

$$\% \text{ error} = \frac{|\text{experimental value} - \text{accepted value}|}{\text{accepted value}} \times 100$$

$$\% \text{ error} = \frac{|30.5 \text{ g/mole} - 28.9 \text{ g/mole}|}{28.9 \text{ g/mole}} \times 100 = 6\%$$

The accepted value of the molar mass of air is 28.9 g/mole.

Teacher Notes

Demonstrate the buoyancy of air by measuring the combined mass of all the syringe parts when the syringe is disassembled. Compare this mass to the mass of an assembled syringe that has been evacuated (step 2 in the Procedure section). The evacuated syringe weighs less than the sum of the parts.

Flinn ChemTopic™ Labs — The Gas Laws

Demonstrations

Teacher Notes

Molar Mass of Butane
Ideal Gas Law Demonstration

Introduction

Avogadro's law, Dalton's law, and the ideal gas law—show how these gas laws can be used to determine the molar mass of butane.

Concepts

- Dalton's law
- Ideal gas law
- Molar mass

Materials

Balance, (0.01 g precision)
Barometer
Pneumatic trough or beaker, 600-mL
Disposable butane lighter

Graduated cylinder, 100-mL
Rubber stopper, size 5
Thermometer

Safety Precautions

Butane is a flammable gas; keep away from all sparks, flames, and heat. Perform the demonstration in a well-ventilated lab and dispose of the gas in a fume hood or outdoors. Wear chemical splash goggles and chemical-resistant gloves.

Preparation

1. Fill the pneumatic trough or a large beaker with room temperature water.
2. Submerge the graduated cylinder in water and fill it completely with water.
3. Submerge the disposable butane lighter in water, remove it, and then dry it off as thoroughly as possible.

Procedure

1. Record the temperature of the water and the barometric pressure.
2. Weigh the disposable butane lighter to the nearest 0.01g and record the mass.
3. Have a student helper hold the inverted graduated cylinder in the pneumatic trough. There should be no air bubbles in the cylinder at the start of the demonstration.
4. Place the lighter underneath the opening of the graduated cylinder and fill it with butane by holding down the trigger. Be careful not to let any of the gas escape around the graduated cylinder.
5. Displace about 90 mL of water from the graduated cylinder. To collect the last 10 mL of butant, adjust the graduated cylinder so that the 100-mL mark lines up with the height of the water in the beaker. Fill the graduated cylinder to the 100-mL mark with butane. By having the graduate in the water at the 100-mL mark, the pressure of gas inside the graduated cylinder will be the same as the atmospheric pressure.
6. Dry off the butane lighter and weigh it again. Record the mass.

The biggest source of error in this demonstration is the mass of the "dry" butane lighter before and after the gas has been measured. For best results, immerse the lighter in water before measuring its mass. Dry it off as thoroughly as possible before and after the gas has been expelled.

Demonstrations

Name: _____

Class/Lab Period: _____

Teacher Notes

Molar Mass of Butane Worksheet

1. Water bath temperature

2. Barometric pressure

3. Volume of gas collected

4. Initial mass of butane lighter

5. Final mass of the butane lighter

6. Mass of butane released

7. What two gases are in the graduated cylinder?

8. Vapor pressure of water (P_{H_2O}) at the water bath temperature

9. Partial pressure of butane: $P_{but} = P_{atm} - P_{H_2O}$

10. Use the combined gas law to determine the volume (in L) of butane at STP.

11. Use Avogadro's law to determine the number of moles of butane gas. Assume that butane is an ideal gas and that one mole has a volume of 22.4 L at STP.

12. Experimental molar mass (g/mole) of butane

13. The molecular formula of butane is C_4H_{10}. What is its accepted molar mass?

14. Percent error using the accepted molar mass of butane

15. Discuss the sources of error in this demonstration.

The vapor pressure of water depends on temperature. Consult a chemistry reference source such as the CRC Handbook of Chemistry and Physics *for the vapor pressure of water at different temperatures.*

Teacher Notes

Sample Worksheet
Molar Mass of Butane

Student data will vary

1. Water temperature: *22° C, 295 K*

2. Barometric pressure: *755 mm Hg, 0.994 atm*

3. Volume of gas collected: *100.0 mL*

4. Initial mass of butane lighter: *22.24 g*

5. Final mass of the butane lighter: *22.01 g*

6. Mass of butane released: *0.23 g*

7. What two gases are in the graduated cylinder? *Water vapor and butane*

8. Vapor pressure of water (P_{H_2O}) at this temperature: *19.8 mm Hg, 0.026 atm.*

9. Partial pressure of butane: $P_{but} = P_{atm} - P_{H_2O}$
   0.994 atm – 0.026 atm = 0.968 atm

10. Use the combined gas law to determine the volume (in L) of butane at STP.
    $P_1 \times V_1/T_1 = P_{STP} \times V_{STP}/T_{STP}$
    0.968 atm × 0.100 L/295 K = 1 atm × V_{STP}/273 K
    V_{STP} = *0.0896 L*

11. Use Avogadro's law to determine the number of moles of butane gas. Assume that butane is an ideal gas and that one mole has a volume of 22.4 L at STP.
    $V_1/n_1 = V_2/n_2$
    0.0896 L/n = 22.4 L/1 mole
    n = 0.0040 moles

12. Experimental molar mass (g/mole) of butane: *0.23 g/0.0040 moles = 58 g/mole*

13. The molecular formula of butane is C_4H_{10}. What is its accepted molar mass? *58.1 g/mole*

14. Percent error using the accepted molar mass of butane:
    % error = |exp – act|/act = 0%!

15. Discuss the sources of error in this demonstration.

    Although the results of one trial, as shown above, were highly accurate, it was found that the results were not very reproducible. The calculated molar mass varied from about 46 g/mole to 74 g/mole over five trials. The major source of error is weighing the butane lighter. A small amount of water will dramatically skew the results. Another possible source of error is the presence of some air in the graduated cylinder before the butane is collected. Finally, some of the butane gas expelled from the lighter may be released into the water bath rather than collected in the graduated cylinder.

Demonstrations

Diffusion of Gases
A Kinetic Energy Demonstration

Teacher Notes

Introduction

The temperature of a gas is a measure of the average kinetic energy of the gas particles. The kinetic energy of any object depends on the mass of the object and on its velocity. Imagine two vehicles—a large truck and a compact car—traveling down the highway at the same time. In order for these vehicles to have the same kinetic energy, the compact car must travel much faster than the large truck. The same analogy can be used to compare the motion of gas particles in different gases at the same temperature.

Concepts

- Diffusion
- Kinetic-molecular theory

Materials

Ammonium hydroxide, concentrated (14.7 M), NH_4OH, 4 mL

Hydrochloric acid, concentrated (12.1 M), HCl, 2 mL

Phenolphthalein solution, 1%, 5 mL

Thymol blue solution, 0.04%, 2 mL

Distilled water and wash bottle

Cotton balls, 12

Glass tubes, 18-mm wide by 30-cm long, 2

Forceps

Latex gloves, disposable

Pasteur pipets, glass, 2

Ring stands and clamps, 2

Rubber stoppers, size 2, 4

Safety Precautions

Concentrated ammonium hydroxide and hydrochloric acid are corrosive and will cause severe burns. Their vapors are extremely irritating, especially to the eyes and respiratory tract. Dispense these reagents in a hood and exercise caution. Phenolphthalein indicator solution contains alcohol and is flammable. Wear chemical splash goggles, chemical-resistant gloves, and a chemical-resistant apron. Please consult current Material Safety Data Sheets for additional safety information.

Procedure

Part A. Diffusion of Ammonia Gas

1. Set up a ring stand and clamp a glass tube in place horizontally.

2. Using a Beral-type pipet, add about 1 mL of phenolphthalein indicator solution to a cotton ball. Set the cotton ball aside to allow the alcohol solvent to evaporate.

3. Hold the "indicator" cotton ball with a pair of forceps and add 10–20 drops of water. Immediately place the cotton ball into one end of the glass tube and seal the end of the tube with a rubber stopper.

4. Using a glass Pasteur pipet, add 10–20 drops of concentrated ammonium hydroxide solution to a clean cotton ball. Immediately place the cotton ball into the other end of the diffusion tube and seal the end of the tube with a rubber stopper.

The time required for the gases to diffuse the length of the tube depends on the tube length. To avoid excessively long diffusion times, use tubes about 30 cm (12 inches) long.

Flinn ChemTopic™ Labs — The Gas Laws

Demonstrations

Teacher Notes

5. Observe how long it takes for ammonia gas to diffuse through the tube and reach the phenolphthalein-soaked cotton ball. *(The front end of the cotton ball will begin to turn pink within about 90 sec. It takes 3–5 minutes for the entire cotton ball to turn bright pink due to the reaction of ammonia with water to form a basic solution.)*

Part B. Effect of Temperature on the Rate of Diffusion

6. Set up two same-sized, clean glass tubes in the horizontal position.

7. Prepare two phenolphthalein-water soaked cotton balls as described in steps 2 and 3. Stopper one ball in place in each of the two glass tubes.

8. Repeat step 4 to prepare two ammonia-soaked cotton balls and stopper one ball in place in the other end of each tube.

9. Heat one tube using a heat lamp, hair dryer, or the soft flame of a Bunsen burner.

10. Compare how long it takes for ammonia gas to reach the phenolphthalein-soaked cotton ball in each tube. *(The cotton ball in the heated tube will turn bright pink within about 45 sec, twice as fast as in the unheated tube. The rate of diffusion increases as the temperature increases.)*

Part C. Comparing the Rate of Diffusion for Ammonia and Hydrochloric Acid

11. Set up two same-sized, clean glass tubes in the horizontal position.

12. Prepare two thymol blue–soaked cotton balls by adding about 20 drops of water, followed by 10–20 drops of thymol blue indicator solution, to each ball. The indicator balls will be dark gold in color. *(Thymol blue is red at pH < 1, blue at pH > 9, and yellow-gold in the pH range 2.8–8.0.)*

13. Stopper one indicator ball in place in each of the two glass tubes.

14. Using a clean Pasteur pipet for each solution, add 12 drops of concentrated ammonium hydroxide solution to one cotton ball and 10 drops of concentrated hydrochloric acid to a second cotton ball. *(Adding unequal amounts of the two solutions compensates for the fact that the ammonium hydroxide solution is more concentrated than the hydrochloric acid solution.)*

15. Immediately place one cotton ball in each glass tube and stopper tube.

16. Compare how long it takes for ammonia versus hydrochloric acid to diffuse the length of the tube in each case. *(Within about 90 sec, the indicator cotton ball in the NH_3 tube will turn blue. It will take about 5 minutes for the indicator cotton ball in the HCl tube to turn red).*

Part D. Gas-Phase Reaction of Ammonia and Hydrochloric Acid

17. Set up a clean glass tube in the horizontal position.

18. Repeat step 14 to prepare ammonia and hydrochloric acid-soaked cotton balls and stopper one ball in place in each of the two ends of the diffusion tube.

Does gravity affect diffusion? Compare the diffusion of NH_3 in a vertical and horizontal tube. If the NH_3 starts at the bottom of a vertical tube, it will travel faster than in the horizontal tube. Is this gravity or density? Challenge your students.

Diffusion of Gases

Demonstrations

19. Observe any changes along the length of the glass tube. *(In less than one minute a white ring of solid NH₄Cl will be visible about two thirds of the way down from the NH₃ source in the diffusion tube. The reaction takes place closer to the HCl source rather than in the middle of the tube because the lighter NH₃ gas molecules travel farther than the heavier HCl gas molecules in the same length of time.)*

Disposal

The cotton balls should be placed in a fume hood to thoroughly degas and then may be disposed of according to Flinn Suggested Disposal Method #26b. Please consult your current *Flinn Scientific Catalog/Reference Manual* for proper disposal procedures.

Tips

- The challenge of this demonstration is handling both the indicator-soaked and ammonia-soaked cotton balls and not contaminating either one. To avoid contamination, always wear clean gloves and hold the cotton balls with forceps.

- The phenolphthalein-soaked indicator balls must be wet with water in order to observe the color change due to ammonia gas. (Ammonia is extremely soluble in water.)

- The concentration of ammonium hydroxide and hydrochloric acid will affect the time needed for the indicator color changes to be observed. It took more than 5 minutes for any color change to be observed for ammonia when the concentration of ammonia was 1 M.

Discussion

Gas diffusion refers to the mixing of different gases throughout an enclosed space due to the random molecular motion of the gas particles. When ammonia molecules are introduced into the diffusion tube, they must mix with the existing oxygen, nitrogen and other gas particles in the tube. The ammonia molecules will collide with other gas molecules and the side of the tube and slowly diffuse down the tube until they dissolve in the water solvent in the cotton balls. The resulting chemical (acid–base) reaction with the phenolphthalein indicator causes a color change from colorless to pink.

The rate of diffusion is controlled by the root mean square speed of the gas molecules. If two different gas molecules have the same average kinetic energy but have different masses, then the lighter molecules will move faster. This is shown in the last demonstration where ammonia molecules (17 g/mole) diffuse faster than hydrochloric acid molecules (molar mass 36.5 g/mole).

The kinetic-molecular theory (KMT) assumes that the particles in a gas are in constant motion and therefore predicts that the gas will eventually fill its container. The KMT also predicts that if two gases are added to a container, they will quickly mix and form a homogeneous solution. The mixing of gases is called diffusion.

Teacher Notes

Demonstrations

Teacher Notes

Construction of Gas Volume Cubes
Assessment Activity

Introduction

According to Avogadro's law, the volume of an ideal gas is directly proportional to the number of moles of gas. Use this "constructivist" activity to help them visualize Avogadro's law and to integrate students' understanding of the gas laws.

Concepts

- Avogadro's law
- Ideal gas
- Molar volume
- Standard temperature and pressure (STP)

Materials

Colored construction paper, at least 45 × 60 cm, 7 sheets
Markers, 7
Meter sticks or rulers, 7
Scissors, 7
Tape, glue or glue sticks, 7

Safety Precautions

Although this activity is considered nonhazardous, observe all normal laboratory safety guidelines.

Overview of the Activity

1. Divide the class into groups of 3–4 students and assign each group a different number of moles of gas from the Assignment Table.

2. Ask each group to calculate the volume that this number of moles of ideal gas would occupy at STP and to construct a cube to represent this volume.

3. Display the cubes for the entire class. The result is an Avogadro's law exhibit!

Assignment Table

Moles of Gas	Volume at STP	Side of Cube
0.00964	0.216 L	6.00 cm
0.0153	0.343 L	7.00 cm
0.0228	0.512 L	8.00 cm
0.0325	0.729 L	9.00 cm
0.0446	1.00 L	10.0 cm
0.0593	1.33 L	11.0 cm
0.0772	1.73 L	12.0 cm
0.0982	2.20 L	13.0 cm
0.122	2.74 L	14.0 cm
0.151	3.38 L	15.0 cm

The moles of gas have been purposely chosen to yield cubes with dimensions to the nearest centimeter. In each case, the number of moles of an ideal gas was calculated by dividing the desired volume by 22.41 L (the molar volume at STP). The results were rounded to three significant figures. Example: A cube with a volume of 343 cm³ (7.0-cm sides) will contain 0.0153 moles of an ideal gas at STP.

Construction of Gas Volume Cubes

Demonstrations

Name: _____

Class/Lab Period: _____

Teacher Notes

Gas Volume Cubes Worksheet

1. Determine the volume in liters (to three significant figures) of _____ moles of an ideal gas at STP.

2. Convert the volume from liters to cubic centimeters (cm³). *Hint:* 1 mL = 1 cm³.

3. Write the formula for calculating the volume of a cube.

4. Determine the length in centimeters of one side of a cube that has the volume calculated in step 2.

5. Choose three gases and calculate their molar masses.

6. Determine the number of grams of each gas that would be needed to occupy the volume of your gas cube. *Note:* Check with the teacher before continuing with the construction project.

7. Using the materials supplied by the teacher, construct a cube having the dimensions calculated in step 4. The cube can be constructed using the pattern shown below or by assembling six identical sides.

8. Record the following information on the six sides (a–f) of the cube. *Note:* This is easier to do before assembling or gluing the final cube.

    a. Names of group members and class period.

    b. Assigned number of moles (step 1).

    c. Volume of the cube in liters and cm³ (step 2).

    d. The number of grams of the first gas that would occupy this volume. Include the formula of the gas, the molar mass, and the grams (steps 5 and 6).

    e. The number of grams of a second gas that would occupy this volume. Include the formula of the gas, the molar mass, and the grams.

    f. The number of grams of a third gas that would occupy this volume. Include the formula of the gas, the molar mass, and the grams.

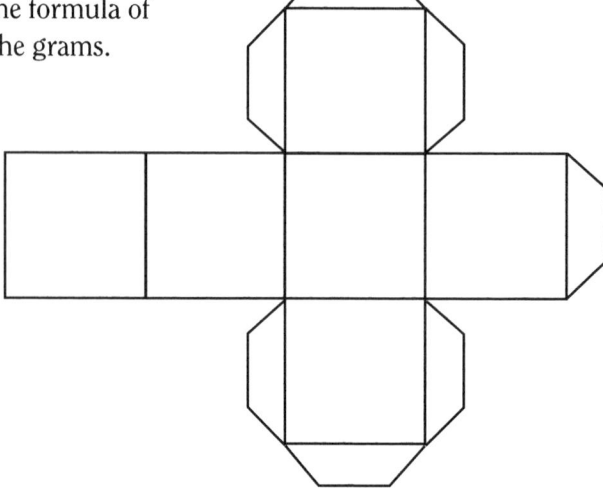

Flinn ChemTopic™ Labs — The Gas Laws

Demonstrations

Teacher Notes

Cartesian Divers
Boyle's Law Activity

Introduction
A variety of squeezable/sinkable Cartesian divers can be made with the simplest of equipment and materials . . . and a little imagination.

Concepts
- Density
- Buoyancy
- Boyle's Law

Materials
Disposable plastic Beral-type pipet
Hex nut, ¼-inch
Plastic soda bottle with cap, 2-L
Beaker, 600-mL
Scissors

Preparation

1. Fill the 600-mL beaker approximately 4/5 full with water.

2. Cut off all but 15 mm of the pipet stem (see Figure 1).

3. Screw the hex nut securely onto the pipet stem. The hex nut will make its own threads as it goes. A ¼"-hex nut works well.

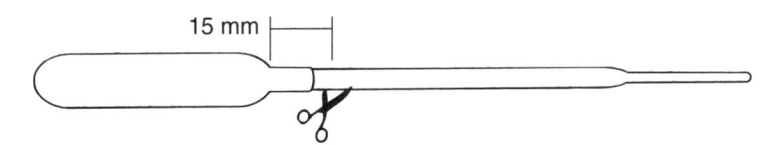

Figure 1. Cutting the pipet

4. Place the pipet-nut diver assembly into the beaker of water and observe that it floats rather buoyantly in an upright position with the hex nut acting as ballast.

5. Squeeze out some of the air and draw some water up into the pipet. Now check the buoyancy. If too much water is drawn into the diver, it will sink. If this happens, simply lift it out of the water, squeeze out a few drops of water and let air back in to replace the water. Using this technique, adjust the amount of water in the assembly so that it just barely floats. (In other words, fine-tune the assembly's density to make it slightly less than that of water.)

6. Place the diver assembly in a plastic 2-L bottle filled with water and securely screw on the cap (Figure 2).

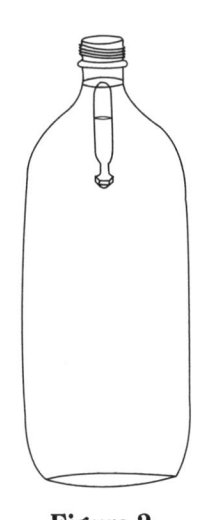

Figure 2.

A "Cartesian Diver Construction Kit" is available from Flinn Scientific (Catalog No. AP9082). Enough pipets and hex nuts are provided to build 100 Cartesian divers.

Demonstrations

Procedure

1. Squeeze the bottle and observe how the Cartesian diver sinks to the bottom.

2. Release the "squeeze" and observe that the diver rises back to the surface.

3. Repeat and ask your students to explain.

Tips

- It is considerably more convenient to adjust the density of the diver and to test for flotation in a 600-mL beaker or in a cup of water, rather than in the bottle itself.

- It is advisable to fill the 2-L bottle completely with water. If the bottle contains too much air, then when the bottle is squeezed, the work will go into compressing the large air space at the top of the bottle and not the smaller air pocket in the diver.

- The demonstration will also work in a glass bottle. For a glass bottle to work, the cap must have an excellent seal, the bottle must be completely filled with water, and the Cartesian diver barely floating.

Discussion

There are really two ways to explain this phenomenon:

1. Consider the diver assembly consists of the pipet bulb, the hex nut and the air and water inside. As the bottle is squeezed, water is forced up into the assembly (because the air pocket inside the bulb is compressible). This adds to the mass of the diver assembly without changing the volume, thus increasing the density of the diver assembly.

2. On the other hand, consider the diver assembly to consist of the bulb, the hex nut and the air inside, but not the water — it is part of the surrounding fluid. As the bottle is squeezed, it compresses the air pocket and thus decreases the total volume of the diver. Since the mass remains constant, the diver assembly's density increases.

Either way, when the Cartesian diver's density increases, it becomes greater than that of the surrounding water, and the diver sinks. When the pressure is released, the compressed air pocket inside the bulb pushes the extra water back out, and the diver assembly assumes its original density and rises to the surface.

Variations

Although the standard diver described above is amusing and educational, the real fun comes in trying some creative variations, such as those listed below:

1. **Cartesian Retrievers.** Place two divers in the same bottle — one that barely floats and one that barely sinks, but with mechanisms or devices attached to them that will enable the floating one to dive down and retrieve the sunken one off the bottom. Use magnets, chewing gum, Velcro, a suction cup, a net, a hook and handle—whatever works! (Figures 3 and 4.)

Teacher Notes

This assembly is formally known as a Cartesian diver after René Descartes, a 17th century French mathematician.

Flinn ChemTopic™ Labs — The Gas Laws

Demonstrations

Teacher Notes

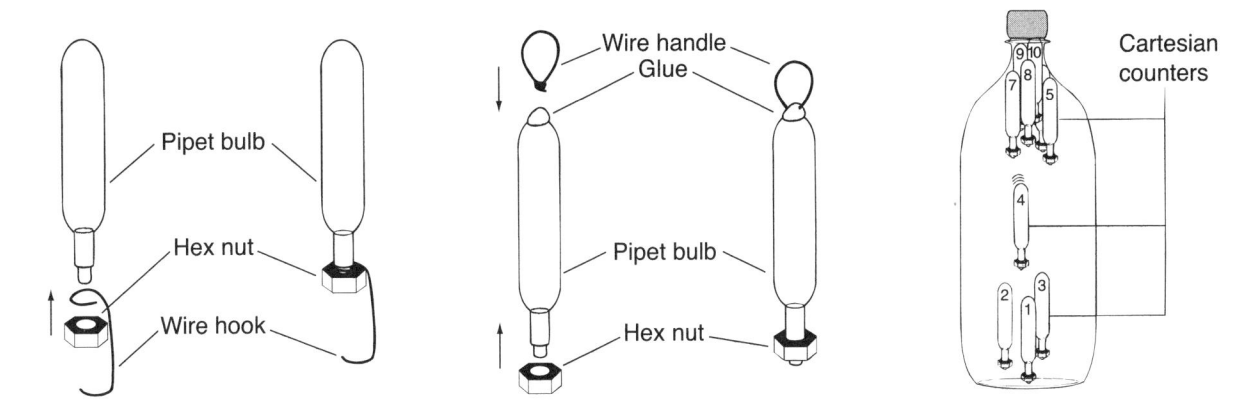

Figure 3. Constructing the retriever

Figure 4. Constructing the treasure

Figure 5.

2. **Cartesian Counters and Messages.** Place several numbered divers together in one bottle, but all with different densities, so they descend in order—1, 2, 3 . . . (or letter the divers to spell out a secret message!) (Figure 5.)

3. **Diving Whirligigs.** Cut a small sheet of plastic into a pinwheel. Punch a hole in the center and fit it onto the stem of the pipet, just above the hex nut. Now the diver will spin gracefully as it sinks, and reverse its spin on the way up. Attach pipe-cleaner arms and legs to make an unusual diving ballerina!

4. **Closed-System Divers.** After the density has been adjusted, try sealing the mouth of the diver with a drop of hot-melt glue. Now, when the bottle is squeezed, instead of water being forced up into the diver's mouth, the sides of the diver are forced noticeably inward (Figure 6). This closed system allows the use of colored water inside the diver and results in divers that can be stored and transported outside the bottle.

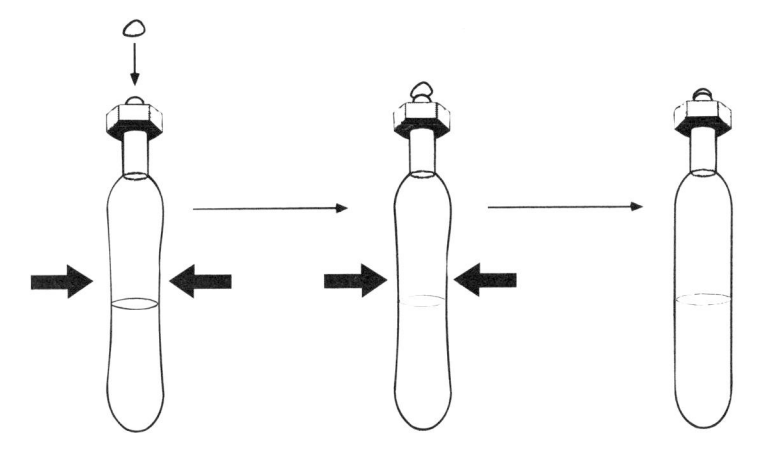

Figure 6. Sealing the mouth of the diver

Cartesian Divers

Safety and Disposal Guidelines

Safety Guidelines

Teachers owe their students a duty of care to protect them from harm and to take reasonable precautions to prevent accidents from occurring. A teacher's duty of care includes the following:

- Supervising students in the classroom.
- Providing adequate instructions for students to perform the tasks required of them.
- Warning students of the possible dangers involved in performing the activity.
- Providing safe facilities and equipment for the performance of the activity.
- Maintaining laboratory equipment in proper working order.

Safety Contract

The first step in creating a safe laboratory environment is to develop a safety contract that describes the rules of the laboratory for your students. Before a student ever sets foot in a laboratory, the safety contract should be reviewed and then signed by the student and a parent or guardian. Please contact Flinn Scientific at 800-452-1261 or visit the Flinn Website at www.flinnsci.com to request a free copy of the Flinn Scientific Safety Contract.

To fulfill your duty of care, observe the following guidelines:

1. **Be prepared.** Practice all experiments and demonstrations beforehand. Never perform a lab activity if you have not tested it, if you do not understand it, or if you do not have the resources to perform it safely.

2. **Set a good example.** The teacher is the most visible and important role model. Wear your safety goggles whenever you are working in the lab, even (or especially) when class is not in session. Students learn from your good example—whether you are preparing reagents, testing a procedure, or performing a demonstration.

3. **Maintain a safe lab environment.** Provide high-quality goggles that offer adequate protection and are comfortable to wear. Make sure there is proper safety equipment in the laboratory and that it is maintained in good working order. Inspect all safety equipment on a regular basis to ensure its readiness.

4. **Start with safety.** Incorporate safety into each laboratory exercise. Begin each lab period with a discussion of the properties of the chemicals or procedures used in the experiment and any special precautions—including goggle use—that must be observed. Pre-lab assignments are an ideal mechanism to ensure that students are prepared for lab and understand the safety precautions. Record all safety instruction in your lesson plan.

5. **Proper instruction.** Demonstrate new or unusual laboratory procedures before every activity. Instruct students on the safe way to handle chemicals, glassware, and equipment.

Safety and Disposal

6. **Supervision.** Never leave students unattended—always provide adequate supervision. Work with school administrators to make sure that class size does not exceed the capacity of the room or your ability to maintain a safe lab environment. Be prepared and alert to what students are doing so that you can prevent accidents before they happen.

7. **Understand your resources.** Know yourself, your students, and your resources. Use discretion in choosing experiments and demonstrations that match your background and fit within the knowledge and skill level of your students and the resources of your classroom. You are the best judge of what will work or not. Do not perform any activities that you feel are unsafe, that you are uncomfortable performing, or that you do not have the proper equipment for.

Safety Precautions

Specific safety precautions have been written for every experiment and demonstration in this book. The safety information describes the hazardous nature of each chemical and the specific precautions that must be followed to avoid exposure or accidents. The safety section also alerts you to potential dangers in the procedure or techniques. Regardless of what lab program you use, it is important to maintain a library of current Material Safety Data Sheets for all chemicals in your inventory. Please consult current MSDS for additional safety, handling, and disposal information.

Disposal Procedures

The disposal procedures included in this book are based on the Suggested Laboratory Chemical Disposal Procedures found in the *Flinn Scientific Catalog/Reference Manual*. The disposal procedures are only suggestions—do not use these procedures without first consulting with your local government regulatory officials.

Many of the experiments and demonstrations produce small volumes of aqueous solutions that can be flushed down the drain with excess water. Do not use this procedure if your drains empty into groundwater through a septic system or into a storm sewer. Local regulations may be more strict on drain disposal than the practices suggested in this book and in the *Flinn Scientific Catalog/Reference Manual*. You must determine what types of disposal procedures are permitted in your area—contact your local authorities.

Any suggested disposal method that includes "discard in the trash" requires your active attention and involvement. Make sure that the material is no longer reactive, is placed in a suitable container (plastic bag or bottle), and is in accordance with local landfill regulations. Please do not inadvertently perform any extra "demonstrations" due to unpredictable chemical reactions occurring in your trash can. Think before you throw!

Finally, please read all the narratives before you attempt any Suggested Laboratory Chemical Disposal Procedure found in your current *Flinn Scientific Catalog/Reference Manual*.

Flinn Scientific is your most trusted and reliable source of reference, safety, and disposal information for all chemicals used in the high school science lab. To request a complimentary copy of the most recent *Flinn Scientific Catalog/Reference Manual,* call us at 800-452-1261 or visit our Web site at www.flinnsci.com.

National Science Education Standards

Experiments and Demonstrations

Content Standards	Boyle's Law in a Bottle	Charles's Law and Absolute Zero	Molar Volume of Hydrogen	Technology and the Forgotten Gas Law	Life on Planet V	The Collapsing Can	Massing Gases	Molar Mass of Butane	Diffusion of Gases	Construction of Gas Volume Cubes	Cartesian Divers
Unifying Concepts and Processes											
Systems, order, and organization	✓	✓		✓	✓		✓			✓	
Evidence, models, and explanation	✓	✓		✓		✓	✓		✓		✓
Constancy, change, and measurement	✓	✓	✓	✓			✓	✓			
Evolution and equilibrium									✓		
Form and function											
Science as Inquiry											
Identify questions and concepts that guide scientific investigation	✓	✓		✓		✓			✓		✓
Design and conduct scientific investigations	✓	✓	✓	✓			✓	✓	✓		
Use technology and mathematics to improve scientific investigations	✓	✓	✓	✓			✓	✓		✓	
Formulate and revise scientific explanations and models using logic and evidence	✓	✓		✓	✓	✓			✓		✓
Recognize and analyze alternative explanations and models											✓
Communicate and defend a scientific argument	✓	✓		✓	✓						
Understanding scientific inquiry	✓	✓	✓	✓	✓		✓	✓	✓		
Physical Science											
Structure of atoms											
Structure and properties of matter	✓	✓	✓	✓	✓		✓	✓	✓		✓
Chemical reactions			✓						✓		
Motions and forces					✓						
Conservation of energy and the increase in disorder		✓		✓					✓		
Interactions of energy and matter											

Flinn ChemTopic™ Labs — The Gas Laws

National Science Education Standards

Content Standards (continued)

Experiments and Demonstrations

	Boyle's Law in a Bottle	Charles's Law and Absolute Zero	Molar Volume of Hydrogen	Technology and the Forgotten Gas Law	Life on Planet V	The Collapsing Can	Massing Gases	Molar Mass of Butane	Diffusion of Gases	Construction of Gas Volume Cubes	Cartesian Divers
Science and Technology											
Identify a problem or design an opportunity											✓
Propose designs and choose between alternative solutions											✓
Implement a proposed solution											✓
Evaluate the solution and its consequences											✓
Communicate the problem, process, and solution											
Understand science and technology											
Science in Personal and Social Perspectives											
Personal and community health											
Population growth											
Natural resources											
Environmental quality											
Natural and human-induced hazards											
Science and technology in local, national, and global challenges											
History and Nature of Science											
Science as a human endeavor	✓	✓									
Nature of scientific knowledge	✓	✓		✓	✓						
Historical perspectives	✓	✓		✓							✓

Master Materials Guide

(for a class of 30 students working in pairs)

Experiments and Demonstrations

	Flinn Scientific Catalog No.	Boyle's Law in a Bottle	Charles's Law and Absolute Zero	Molar Volume of Hydrogen	Technology and the Forgotten Gas Law	The Collapsing Can	Massing Gases	Molar Mass of Butane	Diffusion of Gases	Construction of Gas Volume Cubes	Cartesian Divers
Chemicals											
Ammonium hydroxide (conc), 14.8 M	A0174								5 mL		
Copper wire, 18-gauge	C0148			1.5 m							
Hydrochloric acid (conc), 12M	H0031			83 mL					2 mL		
Helium, lecture bottle	LB1010	1					1				
Hydrogen, lecture bottle	LB1015	1					1				
Magnesium ribbon	M0139			30 cm							
Nitrogen, lecture bottle	LB1020	1					1				
Phenolphthalein indicator solution	P0019								5 mL		
Sodium chloride	S0061	300 g									
Thymol blue indicator solution	T0045								1 mL		
Glassware											
Beakers											
400-mL	GP1025	35	15	15							
600-mL	GP1030										1
1-L	GP1040			15							
Graduated cylinders											
10-mL	GP2005		15								
100-mL	GP2020							1			
Erlenmeyer flasks, 125-mL	GP3040			15							
General Equipment and Miscellaneous											
Balance, milligram (0.001-g precision)	AP9161						1				
Balance, centigram (0.01-g precision)	OB2059							1			
Barometer	AP1884	1		1				1			
Beaker tongs	AP8236					1					
Bunsen burner	AP5344					1					
Clamp, Day pinchcock	AP8211						2				
Clamp, single buret	AP1034			15					2		
Collapsing Can Demonstration	AP4695					1					
Cork borer 12–20 mm	AP1883							1			
Cotton balls	FB0680								12		

Flinn ChemTopic™ Labs — The Gas Laws   82

Master Materials Guide

(for a class of 30 students working in pairs) — **Experiments and Demonstrations**

General Equipment and Miscellaneous, Cont'd.	Flinn Scientific Catalog No.	Boyle's Law in a Bottle	Charles's Law and Absolute Zero	Molar Volume of Hydrogen	Technology and the Forgotten Gas Law	The Collapsing Can	Massing Gases	Molar Mass of Butane	Diffusion of Gases	Construction of Gas Volume Cubes	Cartesian Divers
Felt tip pen	AP1297									5	
Glass demonstration tube	GP9146									1	
Glass tubing cutter	AP5418									1	
Gloves, heat-resistant	SE1031				7						
Gloves, latex	AP4429									4	
Gloves, Zetex™	AP3240					1					
Hot plate	AP4674		5		7	1					
LabPro Interface System	TC1500				15						
Lecture bottle control valve	LB1051	1					1				
LoggerPro Software	TC1421				1						
Massing Gases Demonstration	AP6299						1				
Medicine dropper	AP5102						2				
Meter stick	AP8294									5	
Metric ruler	AP4684		15								
Pipets, Beral-type, graduated	AP1721		30								
Pipet, jumbo	AP8850			15							1
Pneumatic trough	AP8334					1					
Pressure bottle	AP5930	5									
Gas pressure sensor	TC1505				15						
Rubber stopper, one-hole, size 2	AP2302			15							
Rubber stopper, size 5	AP2227							1			
Rubber stopper, size 10	AP2234						1				
Scissors	AP8949			5							
—or— Wire cutters	AP5898										
Scissors, student	AP5394									5	1
Scoop spatula	AP1323		7								
Stopcock grease	AP1095		1								
Support stand	AP8226				15					2	
Syringe, 10-mL	AP1730	5	7								
Syringe, 30-mL	AP1732		7								

Continued on next page

Master Materials Guide

(for a class of 30 students working in pairs)

Experiments and Demonstrations

	Flinn Scientific Catalog No.	Boyle's Law in a Bottle	Charles's Law and Absolute Zero	Molar Volume of Hydrogen	Technology and the Forgotten Gas Law	The Collapsing Can	Massing Gases	Molar Mass of Butane	Diffusion of Gases	Construction of Gas Volume Cubes	Cartesian Divers
General Equipment and Miscellaneous, Cont'd.											
Syringe, 60-mL	AP8754						1				
Syringe tip cap	AP8958	5	14				1				
Temperature sensor	TC1502			15							
Thermometer, digital	AP6049		7	15	optional			1			
Tongue depressors	AP4412		15								
Trays	AP5423				optional						
Tubing, latex	AP2076						8″				
Wash bottle	AP1668				15						
Water, distilled or deionized	W0007, W0001				✓						

Flinn ChemTopic™ Labs — The Gas Laws